THE END
OF
JAPAN INC.

And How
the New Japan
Will Look

CHRISTOPHER WOOD

SIMON & SCHUSTER
New York   London   Toronto
Sydney   Tokyo   Singapore

SIMON & SCHUSTER
Rockefeller Center
1230 Avenue of the Americas
New York, New York 10020

Designed by Edith Fowler
Manufactured in the United States of America

10 9 8 7 6 5 4 3 2 1

Library of Congress Cataloging-in-Publication Data

Wood, Christopher.
    The end of Japan Inc. : and how the new Japan
will look /
Christopher Wood.
        p.   cm.
    Includes index.
        1. Japan—Economic conditions—1989–
2. Japan—Economic policy—1989–   3. Deflation
(Finance)—Japan.   4. Industry and state—
Japan.   5. Japan—Commercial policy.   I. Title.
HC462.95.W66   1994
338.952—dc20   94-28099   CIP
ISBN: 0-671-50145-3

Acknowledgments

The End of Japan Inc. is again the result of numerous conversations. Clearly it is impossible to name all the people who have given me ideas and inspiration. However, thanks are due to *The Economist* for providing me with the opportunity to live in Japan during such dramatic times. Naturally, all views expressed here are my own.

A special thank-you is due to Akio Mikuni, Tadashi Nakamae, Andrew Smithers and Yoshikazu Takao. All four in the past four years have been consistently right in their analysis of the Japanese dilemma in stark contrast to the mass of experts, be they Japanese or gaijin, private sector or public sector, who have been both consistently and spectacularly wrong. Their wise counsel has been invaluable in those moments when the obvious does not seem so obvious amid the numbing conformity of the unthinking consensus. Japan in the early 1990s has not been a fertile ground for conventional thinkers.

Thank you to David Asher, Andrew Ballingal, and Noboru Kawai for reading the raw manuscript and making many worthwhile suggestions. Thank you to Jason Argherinof for working magic with both the hardware and software without which this book would never have been written. Thank you to William Miller, Junzo Sawa, Jan Miller, David Smith

7

ACKNOWLEDGMENTS

and Dominick Anfuso for their enthusiastic support. Thank you to Hiroko Ofuchi and Elizabeth Wollman for everything. Thank you to my family for putting up with the grind of writing. And last but not least, thank you to the Japanese people for being such wonderful hosts during my three-year residence in their delightful country.

TO MY MOTHER AND FATHER

Contents

Note on Foreign Currency Conversion

One dollar was worth 98.5 yen on June 30, 1994.

Based on this exchange rate the following conversion rates apply:

1 million yen = $10,152
10 million yen = $101,522
100 million yen = $1,015,228.60
1 billion yen = $10.15 million
10 billion yen = $101.5 million
100 billion yen = $1.015 billion
1 trillion yen = $10.15 billion

1

No More
Normality

CRUSTACEAN STRUCTURES, however rickety, do not admit defeat so easily. But when they do the subsequent disintegration can be extremely rapid.

On this occasion the admission of failure was certainly a long time coming. It was not until January 29, 1993, that then Japanese prime minister Kiichi Miyazawa finally conceded in response to a question from an opposition Diet member that the collapse of the "Bubble Economy" had occurred. He went on to add that the Bubble's bursting was the first experience of its kind for the Japanese government and that he personally was not aware of what it meant. The aim of this book will be to answer precisely that question. For Miyazawa's remarks were a remarkable admission of defeat for a man whose career personally symbolized the "iron triangle," the nexus of bu reaucrats, businessmen and politicians that had for so long ruled Japan. But far from being made of iron the triangle of late has turned out be composed of some more synthetic substance such as plastic.

The End of Japan Inc. will address the continuing fallout from the bursting of the Bubble, a process that extends from the relatively narrow worlds of economics and finance that were the main subject of the author's 1992 book, *The Bubble*

Economy, to the industrial, political, diplomatic, technological and indeed social spheres. For the crisis that has engulfed Japan in the early 1990s will result in nothing less than the shattering of the country's post-1945 consensus, from which will emerge a new Japan. In fact this process has already begun. Many conventional thinkers will view this assertion as an exaggeration, just as they used to argue wrongly that the impact of Japan's boom-and-bust cycle in the late 1980s would be confined only to those sectors primarily caught up in the speculation, namely finance and property; and that this financial collapse would not affect Japan's "real" economy, be it the virtuous world of manufacturing industry or indeed the willingness of the consumer to spend. It has for some time been impossible to make such claims, as Miyazawa's belated admission showed. For the Bubble's bursting has affected everyone in Japan. The country has clearly become a victim of the same wrenching process of debt deflation that had already been visible for several years in so many other economies. Yet if this process is by now well understood, few people still comprehend that the trauma of debt deflation will be severer in Japan during the 1990s than it has been for the world's other industrialized countries. For Japan faces the reality of outright deflation in terms of falling prices, with all that implies for companies' inability to maintain their profit margins. Japan was facing by the autumn of 1993 an unpleasant combination of excess production capacity, falling demand and a rampantly high yen. Indeed deflation is already happening. Prices fell at a 1.1 percent rate in the first three months of 1993 for the economy as a whole. By August 1993 wholesale prices were declining at an annualized rate of 4.2 percent. This is dramatic stuff. It marks by a wide margin Japan's most severe economic crisis since the American occupation when General Douglas MacArthur set in motion the rebuilding of Japan by surgically implanting a Western-style liberal democracy into a foreign host. That triumph of American colonialism has now more than run its course. The post-1945 model of Japanese economic development was based on the export-driven pursuit of market share in global markets, heavy capital spending and the deliberate suppression of consumer demand. The message of the symbolic collapse of the Bubble Economy is that that form of economic development has now reached its practical limits and beyond. Indeed, the capital spending boom of the late 1980s when business investment reached 22 percent of the gross national product was a lopsided expression of this trend taken to its logical extreme. Key industrial sectors of the Japanese economy have now installed more productive capacity than they need for many years ahead, if not forever.

As a mature economy Japan must now adjust its industrial structure and its society to an era both of slower growth and rapid technological change. For the Japanese postwar economic miracle was built on the national success in mastering the techniques of mass production on the factory floor. This was an area where Japan's conformist and culturally, if not racially, homogeneous society was ideally suited to prosper. However, it is an expertise that now looks increasingly outmoded with the dramatic advances made in computer technology. In the new sort of economy we are now entering, at what to many people must seem a frightening speed, control of the marketplace will increasingly flow away from those who make things to those who control the information. Japan risks becoming the major global loser from this shift from hardware to software precisely because it was the acknowledged champion of mass production. The national stress on conformity and rote learning, bred from infancy up in the education system, may develop skills well suited for manufacturing and attaining a remarkable level of social cohesion. They are a clear liability for stimulating the sort of creativity

17

required in software. But such ominous considerations have only just begun to dawn on Japan's leadership. Yet it takes at least a generation to reform an education system.

If the world is indeed changing in rather important ways, many in Japan are still trying to resist that change, rather like the old-fashioned Luddites in industrializing Britain. Many of the most celebrated features of the post-1945 era in Japan, such as the guarantee of lifetime employment in major companies and the pursuit of market share over profit, were predicated on the rapid economic growth rates to be expected of a developing economy and not on a mature one. Japan was, to borrow the famous analogy, the bicycle economy that had to keep turning the wheels faster for fear of the wheels falling off altogether. Yet so far the response to the economic slowdown from the government has been to try to preserve the status quo as far as possible. In the financial sector, for example, there was a clear move back to re-regulation, which can only be described as reactionary. The most blatant example was the crude rigging of the stock market, where the government ordered public sector financial institutions to buy still grossly overvalued shares with their beneficiaries' money. In the case of the banks this approach took the form of pretending the losses never happened, a form of administratively sanctioned denial. In the industrial sphere companies were actively discouraged by administrative guidance from engaging in the sort of radical restructuring that in many cases was urgently required given the degree of overmanning and labor hoarding. That is widespread layoffs. Instead almost comic palliative measures were adopted, such as ordering employees to stay at home or paying them their bonuses in kind with some of the company's unsold inventory. The perhaps laudable official concern was to preserve the special contract between employer and employee. The failure is to see that this increasingly ossified system is no longer viable if Japan wishes to remain internationally competitive. For there will be no return to "normality," as the bureaucrats still fondly like to describe it. Many Japanese businessmen already understand this. They have to because as practical men of commerce they know what it means to be uncompetitive. While Japanese companies remain for now content to employ more than 3 million excess workers with nothing to do and no value to add, American firms in recent years have restructured ruthlessly. Since 1989 when the U.S. slowdown first became evident American companies have shed more than 7 million jobs in continuing waves of retrenchments, many of them expensive white-collar employees whose jobs will never be replaced as a result of the sweeping advances in information technology. The process may have often seemed brutal. But the penchant for "downsizing" has so far been effective. American companies' earnings have risen, and the American stock market with them during the early 1990s, despite the absence for much of that period of a convincing rebound in final demand. Those companies that have not been able to respond to this competitive challenge promptly enough have failed on a spectacular scale with distressing results in human terms. Witness the dimension of both the financial losses and the job losses at General Motors and IBM. And IBM employees, it should be noted, used to be said to enjoy lifetime employment.

To assume in Japan's case that it can be business as normal in these harsh global competitive circumstances is to assume that Japan can continue to export its way out of recession. This again is naive, and it has become more naive the higher the yen has risen and the larger the trade surplus has grown even if it is true that a large part of the rise in the surplus has been the result of Japan's own domestic slowdown and the consequent steep fall in imports. For the Cold War has ended. Yet too many of Japan's aging politicians have continued to act as if the world's most important bilateral relationship, that between America and Japan, can be conducted as business as usual. This is not the case. The first meeting in Washington in

April 1993 between new youthful President Bill Clinton and aging Miyazawa provided clear evidence that policy in Washington toward Japan will change fundamentally in the coming years. With the end of the Cold War America no longer sees a need or reason to put diplomatic or strategic interests ahead of its own commercial self-interest, as it has done consistently in previous trade disputes since the end of the American occupation of Japan in 1951. And it should never be forgotten that Japan's current prosperity was built not only on Japanese hard work but also on extraordinarily generous access to America's consumer market. Furthermore, Clinton's administration is staffed with results-oriented "managed traders" who are not naturally sympathetic to Tokyo. The Japanese leadership can therefore no longer expect to receive the traditional *gaiatsu* or foreign pressure from Washington for specific measures. This is the sort of highly convenient pressure that Japanese leaders have traditionally found it easiest to respond to. Instead Japan in the future will be expected to come up with measures on its own initiative to reduce the trade deficit, or otherwise face the adverse consequences. This is a demand to which the Japanese leadership, despite recent political changes, will have great difficulty responding. Out of this will result conflict not only between Japan and America but also within Japan between those who argue for preserving the American alliance at all cost and those who will call for reasserting the national self-interest regardless of the breakdown in relations with Washington. This argument will boil down, as do so many long-simmering political issues in Japan, to support for or opposition to Japan's postwar constitution, the essential basis of which was a pacifist foreign policy in return for the American defense umbrella and access to America's consumer market.

Such an argument over fundamentals has already spilled over into the world of domestic politics, marking the end of the post-1945 consensus. For the long-ruling Liberal Democratic Party (LDP) has become a victim of the end of the Cold War just as it was a product of its beginning. America's State Department put the party together in 1955 to cement the anti-communist alliance in Northeast Asia. To this effect Nobusuke Kishi, tried as a war criminal, was rehabilitated as prime minister, since he was viewed by the Americans as a competent and stalwart rightist who would get things done. The LDP served its purpose brilliantly. But its usefulness is now at an end while its legitimacy to rule has been fatally undermined by the domestic economic crisis, the causes of which lay in mismanagement at home, not an external shock such as the OPEC-ordered oil price hike in 1974. Certainly anyone who thinks that the LDP finally lost power in July 1993 only because of the then vogue issue of political reform, as most commentators at the time suggested, needs their head examined. The cause, to borrow a refrain from the last American presidential campaign, was the economy, stupid!

The surest sign that Japanese politics had finally become interesting again after nearly forty years of one-party rule and scant ideological conflict came with the resignation from the Japanese Diet in November 1992 of Shin Kanemaru, then Japan's most powerful politician, and the subsequent breakup of the long-dominant Takeshita* faction within the LDP. Both events it should be noted were predicted by almost no political experts, nearly all of whom took the continuation of the status quo for granted. Kanemaru's downfall was precipitated by prosecutors linking him publicly in court with the late Susumu Ishii, head of Japan's second largest organized crime syndicate and one of the most intriguing underworld figures to emerge out of the Bubble era. Yet the LDP's power has never rested on any claim to moral authority, as is clear from an almost constant succession of earlier corruption scandals. Witness the Lockheed, Recruit and most recently Sagawa

* *Noboru Takeshita was a prime minister who resigned over the Recruit shares-for-favor scandals.*

Kyubin (the one that brought down Kanemaru) affairs. Rather it was based on a record of delivering nearly continuous economic growth. It was that record which was now in tatters, helping to explain Kanemaru's disgrace as Japan's social contract fell apart. The seeds of the LDP's self-destruction lay in the issues raised by the economic crisis, of which the most dramatic is the increasingly urgent need for companies to lay off employees outright, many of them white-collar ones, if they are to remain competitive with American, European and other Asian rivals. For such dismissals will be far more dramatic in terms of their effect on popular psychology than political scandals, however venal, or stock market crashes, however severe. For they will mark the end of a remarkable era in Japan; the post-1945 tradition of lifetime employment or "victimless capitalism" in the country's large- and medium-sized companies. The end of job security, combined with the inevitable (though still fiercely resisted) need to use taxpayers' money to bail out insolvent banks, will generate social trauma, popular discontent and inevitable political conflict. The Japanese polity has already entered a turbulent state of flux as rivals compete to fill the power vacuum left by a disintegrating LDP.

The end of consensus is then clear at many levels. Out of this breakdown will doubtless eventually emerge, this being Japan, a new consensus. But first Japan must deal with the transition at hand. That will prove traumatic, since it will involve making hard choices for a society that has been broadly content to follow the same course for more than forty years. Japan, a country with no centralized political leadership, functions best when the agenda is set and when the broad parameters of that agenda are agreed and understood by the powerful vested interests in society, be they bureaucrats, businessmen, financiers or politicians. Where there is no such consensus the risk of debilitating conflict rises exponentially. The seeds of that conflict are now beginning to appear. It will center on the issue that separated the two major political parties before the militarists rose to power in the 1930s. That is convergence with the West.

The collapse of a political consensus in Japan is clear from the way the two sides have already begun to stake out their positions. After decades of reticence there is a growing willingness in Japan on the part of officialdom and some politicians and academics to assert publicly that Japan has its own different form of political economy, distinct and separate from the Anglo-Saxon tradition of classical economics. Thus, the Ministry of International Trade and Industry (MITI) sought, with admittedly scant success, to influence the Russians following the collapse of communism and the disintegration of the Soviet Union. Two MITI delegations visited Russia in 1992 armed with learned papers about Japan's experience in rebuilding its economy after 1945 and how the policies of industrial planning it used then could be adapted to the Russian case. In other words, Japan's successful example offered a third way between messy free market capitalism and full-scale socialism. That the Western-leaning Russian leadership did not listen probably reflects the enduring antagonism that exists between Russia and Japan, a mutual hostility, which, by the way, should never be underestimated. Still, it is interesting that MITI officials felt sufficiently self-confident even to attempt such an overture.

To adopt a line of argument based on the supposed differences of the Japanese system serves two purposes. First, the Japanese can point to it as a model other developing nations can follow; a useful exercise especially when it comes to reasserting Japan's influence in the Asian region in a way that does not bring back memories of the Greater East Asia Co-Prosperity Sphere of the late 1930s and early 1940s and the rise of Japanese militarism. Second, Japan can use the supposed uniqueness of its own system to counter American demands that it deregulate its economy and financial system more according to classic free market principles.

This view of the Japanese system as different is a feeling that many Japanese like to indulge in if given half a chance. It relates back to their view of themselves as part of a tribal village island society cut off from the rest of the world for much of its history. In this context the modern Japanese company or *kaisha* is seen as a direct successor of the feudal village unit or *mura*. That is, it is a community. The employee belongs to the company but in a spirit of mutual obligation. The ideal is a spirit of enlightened feudalism. The current champion ideologue of this view happens to be one of the Ministry of Finance's top bureaucrats, Eisuke Sakakibara. He is the director general of the International Finance Bureau and a top trade negotiator. Sakakibara is an unusual sort of bureaucrat and indeed an unusual sort of Japanese, which is ironic given his Japan-specific views. He is an outgoing and voluble character, a part-time academic and author who is happy to articulate in several languages what he views as unique about the Japanese system. He therefore states publicly and explicitly what most Japanese would only be comfortable talking about in private, which is why he is not typical. His theory is not particularly complicated but it does make specific what many in Japan view as special about the Japanese way of doing things. The basis of what Sakakibara calls the Japanese model of a mixed economy is "employee sovereignty." In Japan the company is organized around the interests of labor, not of shareholders. As a consequence in America the major factor of production is capital, whereas in Japan it is labor. The basic structure of the economy is held together by companies' reciprocal holdings of one another's shares, the famous system of cross shareholdings that still accounts for nearly 70 percent of the entire Tokyo stock market. Managers are protected from hostile takeovers or indeed dismissal by this cross-shareholding system, especially as on Japanese companies' boards directors and executives tend to be one and the same person. The classic example of this independent feudal corporate kingdom with its own company town as headquarters is Toyota, Japan's premier carmaker, which is based in Toyota City outside Nagoya.

Such is the essence of Sakakibara's vision of Japan's mixed economy. It is clearly far removed from the free market ideal. Sakakibara goes one stage further. He argues that Japan should defend its own system more rigorously against foreigners' complaints about a closed economy rigged against competitors. Ironically, this senior Finance Ministry official sees hope from the fact that the Clinton administration is staffed with people who view the Japanese system as different and therefore will not try to make it conform with American idealistic stereotypes. By contrast, he views the former Republican approach as more ideological. Speaking in his office in the Finance Ministry in the early months of the Clinton administration, Sakakibara said: "If they [the Americans] start saying Japan should become the fifty-first of the United States we will resist." He continued: "We can be partners without making our systems converge. We will retain our culture. We have integrity as a nation." Yet however understandable these comments, Sakakibara's view seems rather naive. What he hails as the "pragmatism" of the new Clinton administration, in the sense of recognizing the perceived differences of the Japanese system, is unlikely to work to Japan's advantage. For the people who argue that Japan is "different" in America, influenced by the so-called revisionist school of thought, are precisely those who call for taking the toughest economic sanctions against Japan in terms of managed trade or even outright protectionism. In fact, Japan could not have had a more sympathetic American administration in the White House than the pro–free traders who were in power during the Reagan and Bush years. That Sakakibara does not under-

stand this is instructive. Also instructive is his failure to explain why the Japanese system has until now proved almost
constitutionally unable to reform itself without the exerting of
foreign pressure or *gaiatsu*. He has written: "It is market
competition, especially international competition, and so-
called *gaiatsu* which have increasingly acted as forces for reform. . . . It is sad in a certain sense that there has been no
large-scale systemic reform without *gaiatsu*, but on the other
hand, it is only normal that it is hard for a stable and successful society to harness the energy for reform from within."*

This is an extraordinary statement. For stable and successful societies do reform themselves from within. Indeed
that is precisely what makes them successful. This is exactly
what foreign governments have long found so exasperating
about Japan. It is a feeling of frustration shared by the more
entrepreneurial and liberal elements within Japanese society
who themselves are now becoming more assertive. For the
other aspect to the coming breakdown of consensus in Japan
is an increased willingness to speak out on the part of those
who look for a greater degree of convergence with the West,
not less. This trend is apparent in the political, business and
even bureaucratic worlds. Japan's younger politicians and
younger bureaucrats are increasingly openly critical of the
performance of their seniors, many of whom they view as
hopelessly out of touch.

An eloquent example of this trend was an article written
by Hiroshi Kumagai and published in Japan's most influential
journal of opinion in March 1993.† Kumagai, aged fifty-two,
was then a leading light of the Reform 21 group of LDP Diet
members, the rebel LDP faction which would later that year
become a new political party and member of the seven-party
non-LDP coalition government in which Kumagai would

* *"The Japanese Model of Mixed Economy: The Anatomy of a 'Non-
Capitalistic' Market Economy."*
† Bungei Shunju, *March 4, 1993.*

serve as a key minister. The leaders of Reform 21 were Tsutomu Hata, a former finance minister, and Ichiro Ozawa, a former LDP secretary general. Kumagai's article is both a scathing critique of the government's failure to react sooner to Japan's economic slowdown and a call for sweeping deregulation of the economy. He attacks heavyhanded administrative guidance and excessive government regulations as stifling the economy. He describes the Japanese system as one of behind-the-scenes "collusion and mutual dealings between politicians, government ministries and companies." Presided over by this iron triangle, the Japanese system has not become a market economy that Japan can be "proud" of. Kumagai goes on to warn that unless Japan deregulates and does more to promote internal demand it risks economic isolation as a result of its seemingly ever-rising trade surplus. For under the present structure the only way out of the domestic recession is to expand exports, risking further conflict with Japan's trade partners. It is up to politicians to seize the initiative, argues Kumagai, since bureaucrats cannot be expected to reduce their own power by curbing administrative guidance. Nor can Miyazawa, himself a former Finance Ministry official. Miyazawa is described scathingly in the article as sitting with "arms folded" doing nothing, yet as "navigator of Japan" he should clearly set the nation's future course. This is powerful criticism especially given the normal deference paid to senior colleagues in Japan, be it in the world of business, politics or the bureaucracy. It becomes more interesting because less than six months later Kumagai became MITI minister in the coalition government, a cabinet position of real importance. He was now in a position to act on his radical views and from his first day in office gave every indication that he would do so. This would hardly please the likes of Sakakibara and his minions over the road at the Finance Ministry.

Nor are pro-deregulation sentiments confined to the younger generation. An equally eloquent example of an attack

on stifling bureaucracy is an article written by Kazuo Inamouri, the founder and chairman of Kyoto-based Kyocera
Corporation, the world's largest maker of ceramic packages
for integrated circuits and one of Japan's most successful companies.* Kyocera is an example of an entrepreneurial company that since its founding in the late 1950s has prospered
through its own efforts rather than by government protection.
The thrust of Kazuo Inamouri's argument is that businessmen
should rebel against regulations when they go against the
interests of the consumer. Deregulation needs to be promoted
not because America or other countries demand it but because it will further the interests of the Japanese people.
Kazuo Inamouri, now in his sixties, also launches a frontal
attack on the bureaucracy. He characterizes officialdom's way
of thinking as one in which "the bureaucracy not only represents the nation but is the nation." He continues: "This bu-
reaucratism, as it is often called, is as different from the
Western brand of democracy as day is from night. As the
bureaucrats see it, the public needs to be closely supervised
and taken care of. They fear that chaos would ensue if the
people were free and left to their own devices."

Anyone with any experience of dealing with the Japanese
bureaucracy would recognize the accuracy of these comments.
The mandarin tradition remains alive and strong in Japan,
especially at the ultra-elitist Finance Ministry, which views
itself and the national interest as essentially indivisible, as one
and the same thing. Yet within the context of this overween-
ing arrogance the bureaucracy is in fact chronically sectional-
ized, as Kazuo Inamouri also points out, with individual
officials seeking to preserve the power of their own individual
ministry and, at a lower level in the hierarchy, their own
bureaus within a ministry and their own sections within a
bureau. As a result, the responsibility of formulating and im-

* Yomiuri, *November 1992.*

plementing policies falls ultimately on the shoulders of those in charge of a section, the subunit of the bureaucracy. The result is a chronic lack of leadership that can result in plain incompetence. Inamouri observes: "Bureaucratic turf is sacred territory. Decision making by consensus is central to this setup. Those in leadership positions cannot thrust their own ideas forward, proposals are formulated at a lower level and while they are being circulated upward the people at the top remain silent. For this system to run smoothly it is best that leadership not be exercised."

These are powerful criticisms from a man who founded and leads one of Japan's most successful companies in the postwar era, and one that is active in the new information economy where Japan needs to excel. They also are light years removed from the sort of arguments in favor of consensus management advocated by Sakakibara. In the chasm that lies between these two views of where Japan should be heading are to be found the seeds of future conflict and the clearest evidence for *The End of Japan Inc.* This is certainly no mere bickering over abstract ideological principles. For even in supposedly pragmatic Japan ideas do matter. Anyone who doubts this assertion need only look back to the last time Japanese society divided over the issue of convergence in the interwar period. It was not a pretty spectacle, and it was this issue that precipitated the rise of militarism and indeed the resulting attack on Pearl Harbor.

The depth and length of the present economic crisis, the inevitability of soaring unemployment in Japan, means that this debate will be joined again. The hope must be that on this occasion, Japan will not seek to stress its differences but embrace convergence. The market route may be messy but it offers the best way of fulfilling the material aspirations of the Japanese people by allowing resources to be allocated efficiently in terms of where they can earn the best rate of return. It also offers the best hope of a less strained relationship with the rest of the world, be it America, Europe or Japan's Asian neighbors. For a renewed obsession with uniqueness will only make Japan an even greater object of suspicion. No one should begrudge the Japanese their cultural heritage and in particular their social harmony, the ultimate expression of which is a nearly crime-free society. And if these traditions are strong enough, and they are, they will continue to survive the continuing inflow of Western multimedia. For Hollywood culture only goes skin-deep in Japan despite superficial appearances to the contrary. But what is dangerous is for the world's second largest economy to stress these differences when it comes to policy making, especially when it has a persistent and large surplus with all its major trade partners.

Japan was throughout the Cold War able to enjoy an ideal halfway house. It was part of this world but also part outside it, a highly convenient arrangement that was only possible because of the protection accorded Japan by the American defense umbrella and the opportunity for growth offered by access to America's wealthy consumer market. But the time is fast approaching when Japan will have to make its own decision about where its future lies. With the end of the Cold War a policy of continued fudge is no longer a practical option. Japan must decide whether to join the world heart, head and soul or to remain oddly unique. In the meantime, the pressures in the real economy will continue to grow, and the political tensions will mount.

2

Politics—
The End
of the Beginning

JAPANESE POLITICS is no longer boring. The tedium of
kabuki has been replaced by the drama of karate. Yet so many
experts had been lulled to sleep by so many years of tedium
they were unaware of the seismic activity that had long been
bubbling away beneath the surface in Nagatacho, Tokyo's political district. Consequently, they were totally unprepared
for the eruption when it happened. For when the long-ruling
Liberal Democratic Party finally lost power in August 1993 it
was as if no one had predicted it. Commentators, who only
weeks earlier had brushed off any such talk as hopelessly
naive because "nothing ever changes" in Japanese politics,
were full of excuses as to why they had not foreseen the
inevitable. The excuses were as lame as they were narrow in
their focus in their concentration on the single issue of political reform as both the catalyst and the cause for change. Such
conventional analysis failed totally to appreciate the full consequences of the end of the Cold War on the Japanese political status quo. For the loss of power suffered by the LDP is
akin to the humiliation suffered by Italy's long-ruling Chris-
tian Democratic Party or indeed the rejection of the communist parties in the former Soviet Bloc. What was at issue here
was the collapse of a ruling order, which gave the appearance

31

of a strong edifice from without but when challenged was revealed to be within tired, rotten and corrupt to the core and without the energy to fight for its own survival.

If most observers failed woefully to understand what was going on there were some exceptions. From an international point of view the author encountered an example of the degree to which foreign critics of Japan have continued to resist fiercely the notion that anything could really change in Japan despite the increasingly overwhelming evidence to the contrary. An op-ed article written by the author and published in the *New York Times* in November 1992* predicting that the LDP would become a victim of the end of the Cold War generated the following illuminating response. The *New York Times* bureau in Tokyo contacted the editor in charge of the op-ed page at the newspaper's head office to complain that the article was completely wrong! It is such reactions that explain why most of the Tokyo-based Western press have massively underreported the biggest story in Japan since the end of the American Occupation, namely the breakdown of the country's post-1945 consensus, and the coming rise of a new Japan.

This enduring conceit—that Japan never changes—increasingly looks less like rational thought than an emotional yearning back to a more simple past without complicating shades of gray. For the reality is that the whole school of revisionist thought on Japan, which has become so influential in American academic, journalistic and now policy-making circles, was built on precisely this assumption. If that is proven false, then the central premise of this whole elaborate pseudoideology collapses and with it much of the rest of the baggage, just as the theory of socialism was disproved by the exposure of what was really going on inside the former Soviet Bloc. In this sense the loss of power suffered by the LDP, coming as it did on top of the economic debacle that has

* *"Japan's Blowup,"* New York Times, *November 11, 1992.*

followed the bursting of the Bubble, has been a severe embarrassment for the revisionist movement. It has not only
proved its adherents to have been hopelessly wrong in their
analysis. But worse it has all but removed their raison d'être,
Japan's supposed difference. This threatens to make them all
but irrelevant.

But in one sense revisionism was not irrelevant. That so
many foreign observers, including many inside Western governments, continued for so long not to recognize the reality of
continuing change in Japan can be blamed on its ideological
influence. Yet the whole revisionist analysis of Japan, with its
collectivist overtones was, to say the least, extremely conde-
scending in its attitude toward what can almost be termed the
natives. For change has been going on for years in Japan,
though admittedly often in a typically subtle Japanese way.
Any remotely observant person, not indoctrinated with revisionist dogmas, should have been able to recognize this if only
by talking to the Japanese people themselves. For thinking
Japanese were more prepared for the possibility of change in
the political status quo than were most of the foreign experts.
One or two even actually predicted it. One of the best examples of this was a paper written in April 1992 by Reizo Utagawa, a former managing editor of the *Mainichi Shimbun*, a
leading daily newspaper, and a fellow of the Tokyo-based
Institute for International Policy Studies. Entitled "Brave
New World: Can Japanese Domestic Politics Change?" Utagawa's paper was as good an analysis as any of the pressures,
or, as he describes it, the "metal fatigue" that caused the
demise of Japan's post-1945 political system. It also happens
to have been brilliantly right.

Utagawa likened Japanese politics to an airplane flying
long after its planned life span has expired. Constant mainte-
nance and patchwork repairs have kept the long-ruling LDP
in power since 1955 but the core material has become brittle
with age. He identified five symptoms of fatigue. First, there

was an absence of debate on substantive policy issues to an extent that amounted to a dereliction of responsibility on the part of career politicians. Second, the LDP itself lacked leadership. Party politics did not work. Instead the LDP had delegated leadership on policy making to the bureaucrats and, as a result, politicians too often became the pawns of high-ranking administrators. Third, the opposition parties engaged in opposition for opposition's sake without any hope or, even worse, desire to assume the responsibility of power. This led to the not so erroneous belief that the biggest opposition party to LDP rule in Japan was the American government. Fourth, the public had long since become cynical and disillusioned about politics as a result of a seemingly never-ending succession of scandals, a fact reflected in the low popularity of ruling politicians and the low voter turnout. The Japanese people were as a consequence alienated from the political process to a far greater degree than in most functioning Western democracies. The fifth and final symptom of metal fatigue was the voracious financial demands placed on politicians. The Japanese political process requires a lot of money. In this sense the politicians are more the victims of the system than the villains of it.

The nature of Japanese money politics requires some explanation. For there is a practical reason for Japanese politicians' seeming willingness to engage in corrupt practices. That is the need to raise money. In other words Japanese politicians are corrupt because the political system breeds corruption, not because they are intrinsically evil people. Consider the following. There are two types of political funding in Japan: *omotegane* (legal or up-front money) and *uragane* (behind-the-scenes cash). *Omotegane* is reported under the political funds control law but *uragane* is not, though it is reckoned to be up to ten times larger. Politicians need this underground source of funding because their constituents demand it of them. Voters expect politicians to pay their respects, literally, at important occasions such as funerals and weddings. And the greater the social rank of the giver the more money he is supposed to give, which means a Diet member often has to hand out the yen equivalent of several hundred dollars on a single gift. The financial demands are increased further by the fact that two candidates from the same party will often run in the same electoral district. In such circumstances there is great competition for votes within the party itself, with the deciding factor as to who wins often becoming an issue of which candidate from which faction can raise the most amount of money to win voter support. Utagawa reckons that the average electoral campaign costs an LDP candidate ¥100 million and the government will only pay one third of that cost. Given the need to tap such vast sums it is not surprising that the ability to raise money has become the chief determinant of political influence and leadership, and not the making of policy. For the politician who can raise a lot of money has the ability to build a faction around him because he can attract the support of other politicians who want a share of his financial spoils. The faction head's control over the money also gives him the power to control key positions, from the heads of Diet committees through to cabinet positions or even the prime ministership itself. Such is the essence of money politics. Utagawa wrote: "First there was money; then factions and policies."

The Takeshita faction, or *Keiseikai*, marked the quintessence of this system exploited to its ultimate extent. The founder of the faction was Kakuei Tanaka, Japan's most famous prime minister in the postwar period and the man who created contemporary money politics. The faction, which used to bear Tanaka's name, controlled the minister-making machine and had chosen every prime minister since the fall of Yasuhiro Nakasone in 1987. The division of the Takeshita faction as a result of the downfall of the LDP's veteran political godfather and Takeshita faction boss, Shin Kanemaru, was therefore the watershed event that future historians will view as the beginning of the end of the LDP. Kanemaru's political downfall was again an event that almost no one predicted until it happened. Yet it became inevitable from the moment in September 1992 when public prosecutors in a statement in court linked him by association with organized crime. The case concerned Sagawa Kyubin, Japan's second largest parcel delivery firm. Sagawa Kyubin ranks with the other most famous scandals of the postwar years, the Lockheed and the Recruit shares-for-favors affairs, which precipitated, respectively, Tanaka's arrest in 1976 and Takeshita's resignation from the prime ministership in 1989. Sagawa may also prove the last of them since it brought down the corrupt system of which it itself was perhaps the ultimate expression. It was a case involving huge sums of money, gangsterism and the murky side of politics. The Japanese people had their first public taste of it with the appearance in court on September 22, 1992, of Hiroyasu Watanabe, the former president of Sagawa's Tokyo subsidiary. Watanabe had been sacked from the company that summer and had been subsequently charged with breach of trust for handing out hundreds of billions of yen in loans and loan guarantees without asking for interest or collateral. The recipients of his largesse were said to include up to two hundred Diet members from both the LDP and opposition parties.

In his opening statement to the court the public prosecutor linked Watanabe—who was denying everything—with Ishii, former boss of the Inagawa-kai, Japan's second largest crime syndicate. Ishii had been a very modern-minded gangster who understood the sophisticated game of finance. He was already notorious, having been previously linked in the summer of 1991 to a different sort of scandal, though another highly publicized one, involving his dealings with Japan's major securities firms. This had led to the resignations of the chairman and president of Nomura, Japan's largest securities firm. Ishii died of a cerebral hemorrhage in September 1991, aged sixty-seven, before he could be interrogated thoroughly on these various matters. Still, by naming Ishii publicly in connection with the Sagawa Kyubin case the public prosecutor badly undermined Kanemaru's already shaky standing.

Such doubtless was the prosecutor's intention. For Kanemaru had only just resigned a few weeks earlier on August 27 from the titular post of vice-president of the LDP after having admitted receiving ¥500 million from Sagawa Kyubin, though the political veteran had claimed in mitigation that the money was actually handed to an aide and not to himself. At the time most cynics scoffed that Kanemaru's resignation from what was only a ceremonial post was all but meaningless. In fact the cynics were totally wrong as they were most of the time during this period of tumultuous change. The prosecutor's linking of Kanemaru by clear implication with the criminal underworld caused by Japanese standards a huge public outcry that grew in intensity as it became apparent not only that Kanemaru was to be allowed special treatment under the law but also that he felt himself entitled to it. It became as a consequence increasingly difficult for Kanemaru to pursue a normal political life. He had become a liability. Accordingly, Kanemaru resigned from the Diet in October in a move that marked the end of his political career, and in the resulting fight over succession the Takeshita faction was rent asunder. Kanemaru protégé Ozawa broke away the same month with finance minister Hata to form their own faction, Reform Forum 21. The mold in Japanese politics had been broken.

So the prosecutor's allegations in open court, where they could be reported freely, had a far-reaching impact. Note that Kanemaru at that time was desperately trying to resist prosecutors' repeated demands that he submit to questioning over the acceptance of his undeclared financial windfall courtesy of Sagawa Kyubin. Japanese law prohibits political donations of more than ¥1.5 million a year. In a bid to make some compromise deal, Kanemaru on September 24 agreed through his lawyers to submit a written statement admitting he received the money. He had already threatened to resign from the Diet if he was charged with breaking the law on political gifts. It was here that his bluff was called with the public linking in court of Watanabe with Ishii. The details of Watanabe's testimony are worth recording since it had such an impact. According to the prosecutor's statement, Watanabe became friendly with Ishii after he asked the gangster in September 1982 to help him suppress a campaign of harassment by an extremist group against Takeshita. Takeshita also happened to be Kanemaru's son-in-law. So, Kanemaru sought Watanabe's help to protect Takeshita. The harassment duly stopped and Takeshita subsequently became prime minister, though he later had to resign the premiership over the Recruit scandal. The prosecutor told the court that Watanabe further developed his relationship with Ishii by lending him huge amounts of money. Ishii used this money to help finance an attempt to corner the shares of Tokyu Corporation, a big railway company. Nomura and Nikko, another securities firm, had already both admitted in 1991 to lending Ishii large sums for the same manipulative purpose. The prosecutor said the gangster gave Watanabe ¥1.7 billion in profits from this speculation alone.

The prosecutor also shed some light on how Watanabe developed his political contacts. Here the link man is said to have been the shadowy figure of Rekiji Kobari, the then seventy-eight-year-old chairman of a bus company called Fukushima Kotsu. Kobari, who was questioned by prosecutors in July 1992 in a Tokyo hospital bed to which he had conveniently retreated, has long-standing connections with the LDP. He is reckoned to have been the main conduit in Watanabe's efforts to buy friends in Nagatacho. But as if all this is not murky enough there is an ever darker aspect of the Sagawa Kyubin case that the mainstream press in Japan has chosen not to discuss and that the prosecutor did not bring up in his court statements. However, it was raised in the September 1992 issue of *Zaikai Tembo*, a financial magazine. The issue disappeared suddenly from the newsstands soon after its publication. The article in question placed the Sagawa Kyubin connection within the context of a group of right-wing nationalists and gangsters active in China, in particular Japanese-occupied Manchuria, before and during the Second World War. Many of the people active in this group subsequently rose to prominence after the war when the occupying Americans decided it was sensible with the onset of the Cold War to put Japanese nationalists in power to counter left-wing influence. The most prominent beneficiary was Nobusuke Kishi. He had been accused of war crimes but the American occupying administration that ran postwar Japan canceled the charge believing that Kishi would prove useful. He became prime minister in 1957. Kishi was head of the Seiwakai faction, which was later led by his adopted son, Shintaro Abe, a former foreign minister who died in 1991.

The old Japan–Manchuria connection is traditionally viewed as hands-off material by Japanese journalists who do not want to have their legs broken or worse, which is one major reason why the Sagawa Kyubin affair has remained so murky. True, Kanemaru, as head of the Takeshita faction, was not part of what is sometimes known as the Manchurian mafia. That was the Seiwakai's connection. But one point is clear. That Kanemaru and Takeshita tapped these fringe rightists both for protection and money was a major cause of their downfall. Less clear is just why they did it, though probably the most mundane reason is the right one, namely the need for money.

The public prosecutor's opening statement may have been enough in itself to inflict the necessary damage. But Sagawa Kyubin–related legal proceedings continued to embarrass Kanemaru and the LDP alike in the months ahead, and these were court proceedings that the press was able to report verbatim. The effect was explosive in terms of keeping Japanese public opinion galvanized. Thus, on November 5, 1992, public prosecutors quoted testimony given by Ryumin Oshima, then head of the Nihon Kominto rightist group, that seven LDP Diet members had asked his group to stop a noisy harassment campaign against Takeshita. The seven named include Kanemaru himself; Yoshira Mori, then chairman of the LDP's policy research council; Keizo Obuchi, recently appointed leader of the remnant of the Takeshita faction left after the breakaway of Ozawa and Hata; Seiroku Kajiyama, then chairman of the Diet affairs committee; plus three lesser-known lawmakers. Prosecutors quoted Oshima as saying that his deceased predecessor, Torao Inamoto, had told him that a proxy for Kanemaru had offered the enormous sum of ¥3 billion as payment for the job of ending the harassment campaign. The politically explosive bombshell came when prosecutors read aloud various testimony in the trial of Munenobu Shoji, president of a company run by the Inagawa-kai.

The same day another embarrassing revelation came out in a deposition taken from Watanabe of Sagawa Kyubin and presented to the court by prosecutors investigating Watanabe's ties with politicians. This was that Kanemaru, Takeshita and then Post and Telecommunications minister Hideo Watanabe had a private meeting with Hiroyasu Watanabe in June 1991 in which they discussed plans to rebuild the by then already financially ailing and scandal-tainted Sagawa Kyubin. According to the document the four met at the home of Kobari, the same Kobari who had been interviewed in his hospital bed. Kobari had advised Watanabe to seek the help of Kanemaru and Takeshita in reviving Sagawa Kyubin's fortunes. The deposition reported Kanemaru as saying he would "talk to the president of Sanwa Bank," and Takeshita as saying he would "talk to Sumitomo Bank as soon as possible" about a restructuring plan for Sagawa. Whatever the exact truth of such testimony, the continuing public revelations of leading politicians' dealings with these fringe characters could only prove hugely damaging.

The public disgust grew as it became clearer that Kanemaru was going to get off lightly for his Sagawa dealings. After much prevarication and doubtless internal anguish, prosecutors finally ended their investigation of the Sagawa Kyubin scandal in January 1993 after deciding not to charge Kanemaru with violating the political fund control law. As a result, Kanemaru ended up paying only a ¥200,000 fine for receiving an illicit donation in what was technically classified as a summary indictment. This meant he did not have to undergo the embarrassment of a public trial. However, this special treatment for Japan's leading politician was so brazen that it ultimately sowed the seeds of Kanemaru's personal downfall as the normally compliant Japanese news media, including television, howled its outrage at the deal that had been struck.

Kanemaru's political career may have been at an end. But he now faced the worse prospect of personal humiliation and even incarceration. For with their professional pride hurt, if not humiliated by the public outcry that they had let Kanemaru off virtually scot-free, the prosecutors were in no mood to be lenient when tax investigations soon led to an even more damaging case against Kanemaru. The story broke in March 1993 when the special investigation squad of the Tokyo district public prosecutor's office arrested both Kanemaru and his aide, Masahisa Haibaru, on suspicion of income tax evasion. The noteworthy point here was the sheer amount of money involved in supposedly egalitarian Japan. Following raids on Kanemaru's home and offices, prosecutors found in safes and other various nooks and crannies bank debentures worth ¥5 billion plus another ¥1 billion of gold bullion and cash. These were huge amounts for a political fixer not known for his business or financial acumen. They also represented wealth Kanemaru had neglected to inform Japan's fierce tax authorities about. As a result, Kanemaru was charged with evading hundreds of millions of yen in tax.

The sums were gargantuan by the standards of Japanese salaried men and were again explosive in terms of their negative impact on Japan's fraying social contract. Kanemaru's political career may have already ended as a result of his resignation from the Diet. But his figure was so personally associated with LDP rule that his public disgrace could only further seal the ruling party's fate. It also meant an astonishing plunge in personal fortune for Kanemaru. The former political godfather was treated like a common criminal suspect. With memories still so fresh about the way he had got out of the Sagawa case, Kanemaru was allowed no special treatment. Despite his age he was held for questioning in a small solitary cell in the Tokyo Detention House equipped with just a futon mattress and toilet. Naturally the Japanese press dwelt on these juicy details of the personal comeuppance of a man who is likely to go down in the record books as the biggest tax evader in Japanese history.

The political downfall of Kanemaru gave Miyazawa, whom the don had put in office, the opportunity to try to shape his own administration. For this reason the first half of 1993 saw the LDP fall back under the rule of bureaucrats-turned-politicians since Miyazawa had entered politics from the Finance Ministry. It was a doomed attempt by the old order to reestablish control of the political process from the pork barrel politicians of whom Kanemaru was the personal embodiment. The initiative failed because the aging men in charge showed a failure of historical imagination. They thought that the only issue which mattered was eradicating the worst excesses of money politics. They failed to understand that more thorough reform was needed, both in terms of political restructuring and deregulation of the economy; that the old bureaucratic-shaped policy of an economy based on capital spending and pursuit of exports no longer worked.

Consequently, their policy response was woefully inadequate since their central assumption, that it was business as normal, was wrong.

Still, this temporary return to political influence of the ex-bureaucrats did have one significant impact. It put in charge of the judicial process a man who personally assured that the purging of Kanemaru would be pursued all the way to full-scale prosecution of the former political supremo. This was the veteran inside operator, Masaharu Gotoda. Gotoda was appointed justice minister by Miyazawa in December 1992 in a cabinet reshuffle. The following April he was also made deputy prime minister after the resignation from that position of then foreign minister Michio Watanabe, who was sick with stomach cancer. It is clear that Gotoda had by then decided that there was an urgent need to clean up Japanese politics and in particular the LDP. Prior to his appointment Gotoda had been heard to deplore the influence of money politics, and he clearly wanted to do something about it. This he subsequently did, which is why for a few months it was no exaggeration to describe the then seventy-eight-year-old as the most important man in Japanese politics. For it was Gotoda who personally authorized the prosecutors (who reported to him as justice minister) to indict Kanemaru on the tax evasion charges after the public outcry that followed Kanemaru's being let off criminal prosecution after he had admitted to accepting ¥500 million from Sagawa Kyubin.

However, Gotoda was no reforming radical. He was in fact an arch-conservative with a strong belief in a strong Japanese "state." He had no wish to undermine the status quo he represented, namely the bureaucratic-political nexus that formed one key part of the LDP. Indeed, his purge of Kanemaru was an attempt to try to defend that status quo before a combination of continuing corruption and public revulsion destroyed it. Gotoda's attitude was natural given his background. A former bureaucrat and intelligence and security expert who had worked before the Second World War for the subsequently disbanded *Naimusho* or Ministry for the Interior, then Japan's most powerful ministry, and after the war for the National Policy Agency, Gotoda had a reputation for both toughness and integrity. He was also a political survivor par excellence, having served at various periods as director of the National Policy Agency, as deputy chief cabinet secretary (the highest post for a career bureaucrat) under Tanaka, and as chief cabinet secretary under Nakasone. It is worth noting that Gotoda is reputed to have been the only person the formidable Tanaka respected, or rather feared. This was partly due to his steely nature and also partly because, as a former police chief, he had information on everyone. Gotoda soon confirmed his reputation as a hard man in a very public way on taking over the Justice Ministry. He gave the go-ahead for the execution of three men who had been on death row for years. Preceding justice ministers had in typical Japanese fashion preferred to defer on such a sensitive issue. But for Gotoda this was not a relative matter. Rather, it was simply an issue of enforcing the law as it stood and thereby upholding the authority and integrity of the state.

Gotoda's new power base raised much speculation as to who among Japan's famously venal politicians he would authorize the prosecutors to go after next. Certainly most observers assumed there was evidence available to launch similar cases to Kanemaru's if the political go-ahead was given. For when the men from the Tokyo public prosecutor's office ransacked Kanemaru's home, office and political headquarters, they found a ton of incriminating evidence in addition to those large holdings of discount bearer bonds. Further probing led to the companies that bought these anonymously owned bonds. They turned out to include major construction firms such as Kajima, Shimizu and Taisei. The investigating prosecutors subsequently raided the offices of these firms and questioned their senior officials. They uncovered more detailed evidence of payments made to virtually every major LDP politician in Japan. Japanese press reports spoke of "unaccountable expenditures" for Kajima, Shimizu and Taisei amounting to ¥15 billion in 1990 and 1991 alone. The donations reflected the pecking order among politicians. Thus, Shimizu considered it was worth paying Kanemaru and Takeshita ¥10 million each twice a year, whereas former prime minister Toshiki Kaifu or LDP rebel Tsutomu Hata were only considered worth paying ¥3 million per time (twice per year).

As in post–Cold War Italy where institutionalized corruption on a grand scale was also being exposed at the same time, none of this came as any great surprise to the populace at large. The construction industry has long been regarded as the biggest source of funding for the LDP. Still, it was one thing to suspect such activities and quite another to have detailed evidence documenting it, especially if there was powerful political support for prosecutors actively to pursue the matter. This helps explain the (for Japan) extraordinary public row that broke out in April 1993 over the position of Rokuro Ishikawa, chairman of Kajima, as then chairman of the Japan chamber of commerce. Kajima is Japan's most blue-chip construction firm. Yet to its intense embarrassment it had had its offices searched along with the other construction riffraff. This spectacle caused leading businessmen to call for Ishikawa to resign from his position at the chamber of commerce. Most outspoken was Nissan chairman Yutaka Kume. He made it very clear he wanted Ishikawa out, going so far as to accuse the construction industry in public of "lying" by denying its widespread practice of illegally donating funds to politicians in return for favors. That the Japanese government had then just announced its second major supplementary budget within nine months, major beneficiaries of which through the award of public works contracts would be construction firms, only made the issue that much more topical. Ishikawa initially stonewalled. But he duly resigned later in the year after remaining in office for a few face-saving months.

This did not mean an end to construction-related probes. Gotoda is no longer justice minister with the fall of Miyazawa's government (and besides he had a bad heart attack in the summer of 1993, which would have put him out of active political life anyway even if the LDP had clung to power), but Japan still experienced the equivalent of an "Italian Job," with a series of leading public figures resigning in construction-linked scandals stemming from evidence obtained as a result of the Kanemaru case. The areas targeted included the involvement of municipal governments in *dango* or bidding cartels in the construction industry. To cite just two examples the mayor of Sendai has been arrested as has the chairman of Shimizu. Two likely future targets are the local governments of Chiba and Yokohama outside Tokyo, both of which saw mega-construction projects during the Bubble era. The point always to remember is that just because there is a seeming lull in prosecutors' activity does not mean that an investigation is at end. That is certainly the lesson to be drawn from the Sagawa Kyubin case, which first began to attract public attention in 1991 long before the move against Kanemaru.

Two of the leading politicians most commonly reckoned to be in danger of prosecution from Kanemaru-linked investigations are Ozawa and Takeshita. Neither is likely to leave as much incriminating evidence lying around as the rather unsophisticated Kanemaru. However, both were extremely close to the former don. But in one key sense they are different. Takeshita represents only the past of Japanese politics. Ozawa is both the past and the future. For this reason Ozawa may well prove to be the key man in Japan's coming political realignment. He is certainly the man most instrumental to date in bringing about the collapse of Japan's post-1945 political consensus. He is also one of the few politicians today who has a clear vision about what should replace that shattered consensus.

A complex man, Ozawa is a machine politician who knows the intricacies of money politics as well as anyone, yet has a reputation as a reformer. He learned his LDP politics in the best way possible, namely at the center of the then Tanaka faction. The son of a four-time cabinet minister, Ozawa following his election to the Diet in 1969 became Tanaka's personal protégé and almost his surrogate son. The old man and giant of Japanese post-1945 politics presumably saw in Ozawa a younger version of himself. After Tanaka fell from power with the Lockheed scandal Ozawa grew closer to Kanemaru (though Tanaka did not ultimately lose control of the faction to Takeshita until 1987) Ozawa had earned Kanemaru's favor because in 1983 he had suggested to Tanaka, who still dominated faction affairs though he was no longer prime minister, Kanemaru's appointment to the key post of LDP secretary general. Kanemaru returned the favor when in 1989 he had Ozawa made secretary general in the administration of Toshiki Kaifu at the (by LDP standards) young age of forty-nine. The only other LDP politician to have reached this position at a similarly young age was Tanaka himself. The post of secretary general is commonly viewed as a training ground for the prime ministership.

Ozawa has many of the qualities necessary for Japanese politics, most notably a facility for raising funds and playing the game of money politics. This is why there remains a clear risk he could be implicated in a Kanemaru-related investigation; that he could be brought down by the corrupt system he now says he wants to reform. But Ozawa has another side to his political personality. Like Nakasone before him, Ozawa is unusual among Japanese politicians in that he is not afraid to speak his mind and go up against the bureaucrats. It is this quality that explains why American officials who worked with him during the Bush administration say they were most comfortable negotiating with Ozawa out of all Japan's leading politicians. He was certainly no pushover. But because he had the confidence to take a position and negotiate an agreement he was a man it was possible to deal with. For similar practical "can-do" reasons Ozawa tends to be popular with the Japanese business community, a fact that has helped him raise funds after he departed the LDP.

Also, like Nakasone before him, Ozawa believes in a more politically self-confident Japan equipped with its own independent foreign policy. When the Gulf War broke out in 1990 Ozawa was the leading agitator for a more activist role. Indeed, he saw the conflict as an opportunity to break fundamentally with the long-standing purely pacifist interpretation of Japan's postwar constitution. And as LDP secretary general he was instrumental in knocking heads together to ensure that Japan made some form of financial contribution to the Allied cause.

So Ozawa is certainly no woolly-headed liberal. Yet he is a genuine reformer despite his background in LDP machine politics. He is a reformer because he realizes the old system has broken down; that it no longer works. His views were well expressed in an interview with *Nikkei Business* held in July 1993 shortly after the fall of the Miyazawa government but before the formation of the coalition government in which Ozawa, though not a cabinet member, was the key figure pulling strings backstage. Ozawa stated clearly in this interview what he felt was wrong with the old Japanese system, and it was clear he was talking about much more than just the single issue of electoral reform. Indeed, he went so far as specifically to advocate an end to politics by consensus. He said: "One-party rule, collusion between the ruling and opposition parties, and close ties among politicians, bureaucrats and the business world caused Japanese politics to stagnate." What was now required was to restore the tension bred by competitive politics. "It is vital to revive a basic element of parliamentary politics, the atmosphere of tension present when there is a possibility of the government's changing hands." For the old system was designed in such a way as to prevent politicians making any decisions. Ozawa continued: "The most serious problem was the lack of ability to make decisions. In the LDP decisions must be unanimous. This is impossible in a democracy. In the LDP, nothing gets decided, and no one takes responsibility." Clearly, in Ozawa's view this is the opposite of leadership.

Ozawa has also been extremely specific in terms of his policy proposals. They are explained in his best-selling book, *Nihon Keizo Keidadi (Reforming Japan)*. These make it clear that Ozawa realizes, despite his own background as a Diet member for a rural constituency, that the new political party he is effectively leading has to represent the interests of the vast ranks of salaried men, the urban and suburban consumer. Thus, Ozawa is in favor both of a dramatic halving of income tax and cutting the corporation tax from 37.5 percent to 33 percent. These two measures would be paid for by increasing the consumption tax from 3 percent to 10 percent. Such a shift from direct to indirect taxation makes eminent sense. Japanese employees have far too much of their pay deducted straight from their salary. Greater disposable income would in the long run promote a more consumption-oriented economy. It would also give people an incentive, reducing the unhealthy tendency among office workers to base their life around their company expense accounts. Such a fundamental tax reform is naturally anathema to conservative bureaucrats who think that they are better guardians of the people's hard-earned money than the people themselves.

So Ozawa is as well placed as anyone to forge Japan's new politics assuming (a major if) he can avoid criminal prosecution. His political tactical sense has also been further displayed in his choice of a major ally, Hata. This is a classic example of the good guy–bad guy routine. Ozawa is the political operator, the thug who stays in the background, raising money, negotiating deals with opposing parties and factions and generally working the system. Hata is the acceptable front man with strong popular support and a good television presence. Furthermore, Hata is genuinely sincere about his belief in political reform. Unlike Ozawa, whose political career within the LDP was jeopardized by the fall from grace of his mentor, Kanemaru, Hata had no reason to give up the key Finance Ministry post in the Miyazawa government (he had previously served as agriculture minister) to split off with Ozawa. He therefore took a major gamble with his political career because he believed in the need for a realignment of Japanese politics. The usual cynical media commentators have suggested that Hata is merely a stooge for the more powerful Ozawa. This is to exaggerate. Ozawa has needed Hata perhaps as much as Hata has needed the politicking skills of Ozawa, since he lent the Reform 21 movement an integrity of purpose that was fundamental to its credibility.

This is why the greatest threat to Ozawa's plan to break up the LDP came in April 1993 when the LDP leadership tried to persuade Hata to take the Foreign Ministry post in Miyazawa's government following the resignation on grounds of ill health of Michio Watanabe. The plan cooked up by Gotoda and then LDP secretary general Seiroku Kajiyama was a deliberate ploy to break up Reform 21 and, by luring Hata back within the fold, to bolster the LDP's own reform credentials. The offer was made on April 6 when Miyazawa spoke to Hata over the phone after Hata had finished a morning television show. Frequent TV appearances by the likes of Hata have been a growing feature of Japanese politics since the splintering of the Takeshita faction. The rebels needed a public outlet since they were no longer inside the club. At a meeting later that morning of the rebel LDP faction the majority voted overwhelmingly against Hata taking the Foreign

Ministry job. Hata duly turned it down, though later that same day, according to *Tokyo Insideline*, a monthly publication, both Miyazawa and Gotoda had extensive phone conversations with Hata seeking to persuade him to accept. But fortunately for Ozawa, Hata remained loyal to his fellow rebels. This was one of the two moments of truth for the Ozawa-Hata breakaway group. The second would occur less than three months later with the failure of Miyazawa's political reform bill.

The problems may have long been fermenting in terms of policy paralysis and an inability to make decisions. But when the crack-up of the LDP finally came, its cause was gross political incompetence on the part of then prime minister Miyazawa. This was appropriate since Miyazawa personified a political order dominated by ex-bureaucrats to which both Ozawa and Hata were so strongly opposed. He also showed an older man's failure to understand what was really going on around him. A creature of the postwar settlement, Miyazawa simply did not understand what was at stake. As such he was crushed between those forces pushing for electoral reform and those within his own party who wanted nothing to do with it.

Miyazawa made one major mistake, which precipitated his downfall and the LDP's subsequent loss of power. This was his public pledge that he would push through some form of electoral reform bill by the end of the main 1993 parliamentary session. This was extremely unwise since he could not have been sure he could personally garner the necessary parliamentary support to bring about this result. In other words he promised something he could not definitely deliver. An elitist mandarin figure with a penchant for outdated Keynesian economics, Miyazawa was not the man to cut deals in smoke-filled rooms. Indeed, he did not really bother to consult with people in the LDP at the Diet floor level. This meant he had little idea of how opinion was running within the party. It also meant that he did not understand the extent to which many in the LDP regarded him as dispensable despite the threat posed by the breakaway Ozawa-Hata group.

The immediate trigger for Miyazawa's humiliating failure over political reform was a secret May 1993 meeting attended by Nakasone and Kajiyama, plus a handful of others, at which it was decided that the time had come to get rid of Miyazawa. For Miyazawa actually seemed serious about trying to introduce substantive electoral reform just as the unfortunate Kaifu had been before him, an aim in which he was supported by the powerful Gotoda, who saw such reform as a necessary mechanism for eradicating the worst aspects of money politics. The secret LDP plotters viewed this with alarm, since real reform would undermine the power-broking system of factional politics, which was both the source of their influence and the only game they knew how to play. Accordingly, it was decided to spoil Miyazawa's efforts to push a political reform bill through the Diet and thereby undermine his premiership. The chief spoilers would be Kajiyama, acting for his political boss, Takeshita, and Sato, acting for his boss, Nakasone. Ozawa, astute political tactician as he is, smelled the wind and sensed an opportunity. He prepared to marshal his forces.

Meanwhile Miyazawa, seemingly oblivious to the threat surrounding him, continued to insist publicly that he would push through political reform. Either he was naive or he had begun to think he could act independently of the likes of Takeshita and Nakasone, an act of faith that if true can only be described as a delusion. This was despite Kajiyama's growing hints to the prime minister to let the political reform bill expire unpassed in the current parliamentary session. Miyazawa continued to refuse to take the hint, an attitude that caused Kajiyama to go public on June 14 when he told a meeting of the Keidanren, Japan's major employer group, that he hoped political reform would occur after the LDP had won the upper house (Diet) election in "two years' time"! This astonishing statement was, of course, a way of saying political reform would not happen now. It caused an outcry in the reformist Ozawa-Hata camp and it left Miyazawa out on a limb, since he had committed himself so publicly to passing some form of electoral reform in this particular Diet session. This was an odd state of affairs indeed. Commenting on it, Yoshinari Yamashiro, chairman of the major steel company NKK, told the Japanese magazine *Ekonomisuto* shortly after the political drama had occurred that the LDP, as represented by the stance taken by Kajiyama, and the prime minister seemed to be heading in "totally opposite directions." He added that it was the LDP that destroyed Miyazawa's reform plans.

This was indeed the right conclusion. But the plotters miscalculated badly. The LDP was no longer the tightly disciplined machine it had been when the Takeshita faction ran everything, such as when Kaifu's premiership was swiftly curtailed by Kanemaru in late 1991 when that former prime minister became too enthusiastic about political reform and began to think he could act independently of the political machine. For by undermining Miyazawa in so humiliating a fashion Nakasone and Takeshita gave Ozawa the opportunity he had been waiting for.

The collapse of the effort to pass political reform enabled Ozawa and others of his rebel faction to go on television accusing the LDP and Miyazawa of breaking their promise. This shamed the traditional opposition parties into action, some of whom, in particular the socialists, did not really want a dissolution and a general election at all because they were in no condition to fight one. The result was a tabling of a no-confidence motion by the socialists and other opposition parties. It was the loss of this motion on June 18, caused by the Ozawa-Hata group voting against the LDP, that brought down the Miyazawa government and the calling of a general election. The attempt to restore government by ex-bureaucrats was over as indeed was rule by the LDP. For the losers included not only Miyazawa but also Nakasone and Takeshita, who had believed they as senior power brokers could still manipulate events from behind the scenes. Kajiyama and Sato had only been serving as noncommissioned officers doing their generals' bidding. They were not made of the stuff that could save the LDP.

If the issue of political reform was the catalyst for these dramatic events, there was clearly far more at stake than just tinkering with the electoral system. Ozawa himself in typically frank fashion has made this brutally clear, even in discussions with the foreign press. Thus, he told the Hongkong-based *Far Eastern Economic Review:* "Electoral reform is not our ultimate objective. Our aim, rather, is to transform postwar Japanese politics itself."* It is hard to be more direct than that. Still, electoral reform is far from unimportant since it will change the way Japanese politics works, which is why many traditionalist LDP members representing rural constituencies continued to resist it despite the obviously strong public support for reform of the system.

The main plank of electoral reform was the proposal to change the system of medium-sized, multi-member electoral districts. Under this system there were 511 MPs elected to the lower house of the Diet. Note a key point. These districts had not been adjusted for population movements. This was the reason for the substantial overrepresentation of the rural vote. In the urban areas the minimum number of votes required to get elected was about 80,000. In a rural district it could be as low as 35,000. But the size of constituencies was not the only component of political reform. The other issue was the type of electoral system to be adopted. Out of this debate emerged a general agreement among pro-reformers and LDP rebels that the reformed system should be a com-

* *July 1, 1993.*

bination of first-past-the-post "small" electoral districts where the winner takes all and a nationwide "list vote" where seats would be allocated by proportional representation (that is, in direct proportion to the percentage of votes received). This will probably break down into 250 MPs elected from small districts and 250 by a national party vote. Whatever the exact details of the final legislated outcome, and the proclaimed priority of Japan's new coalition government is electoral reform if only because it is about the one policy on which all its diverse members can agree, its passage will go a long way to ensure a political system better representing the interests of the urban consumer. The long-term importance of this in forging the new Japan is hard to exaggerate.

So political reform proved the trigger for the downfall of Miyazawa and the open rebellion of Ozawa and Hata, who promptly formed their own political party, the Shinseito or Japan Renewal Party, to prepare for the upcoming general election. Hata was the nominal leader but it was Ozawa who had the job of building an electoral machine in a hurry. But Shinseito was not the only political party with reformist credentials out there competing for votes. Others had made their move earlier, most notably Morihiro Hosokawa, the fifty-five-year-old former governor of Kumamoto Prefecture in Kyushu, the island south of Honshu. Hosokawa had formed his Japan New Party a year previously under the twin banners of local autonomy and political reform. He therefore had a machine up and running, which was a great help when it came to election time, as indeed proved to be the case in the Tokyo council elections held at the end of June just three weeks before the general election.

This local poll turned out to be a near perfect forerunner of what was to occur in the national poll. The Tokyo election results confirmed that Japanese politics was indeed in a state of flux. But the startling point was not the relatively strong showing of the LDP but the collapse of the socialist vote. The

Social Democratic Party ended up with only fourteen seats in the new Tokyo legislature compared with twenty-nine held previously. This poor performance made total sense. For the socialist party was as much a feature of Japan's imploding post-1945 political order as was the LDP. Its role during the Cold War years was that of token opposition. The party's still strong pacifist beliefs also meant that the socialists played a useful role throughout this period blocking any attempt by more nationalist elements within the LDP to redraft the 1952 Japanese constitution and amend the security arrangements with America. Nationalists have always considered this status quo humiliating, arguing, not so unreasonably, that it reduced Japan's national status to that of a mere protectorate. The socialists' electoral failure meant that they would now have to move sharply to the right if they wanted to survive, and that the traditional left wing would not be a part of political re-alignment in Japan.

The other feature of the Tokyo election was the strong showing of Hosokawa's Japan New Party, which won twenty out of the twenty-two seats it contested. This gave it considerable momentum going into the general election, whereas the Japan Renewal Party (Shinseito) had to fight the election virtually from scratch, though it is true that most of its candidates were former Takeshita faction Diet members and so experienced politicians. This was not the case with the Japan New Party. Its candidates included television commentators and similar yuppie types employing almost American-style campaign techniques in what was a much needed breath of fresh air by the staid standards of Japanese electoral campaigns. Still, the colorful cosmetics did not disguise a lack of substance. Serious doubts remained about Hosokawa himself. Scoffers said at the time that he and his party had no policies and would prove a temporary fad. That was a little too glib. Hosokawa has a pretty face, which is not unimportant in the world of TV sound-bite politics. He also hails from one of

Japan's most aristocratic families, which also helps. Mr. Hosokawa is descended from the long-ruling samurai family of Kumamoto prefecture.

The Hosokawa group received another boost with the disclosure following the Tokyo election that it was linking up with the only just formed Sakigake or New Harbinger Party, led by yet another LDP defector, Masayoshi Takemura. Like Hosokawa, Takemura was a former provincial governor with genuine reformist credentials. He had served as secretary general of the LDP's political reform headquarters for five years.

Takemura was illuminating in an interview published in the *Chuo Koron* in September 1993 as to the reason why he allied with Hosokawa rather than Ozawa and Hata. He said that Hosokawa's party was "literally pure white" while the Shinseito was organized like an LDP faction with the obvious model the Takeshita faction. Takemura said: "The group has an army-corps-like constitution. . . . It is virtually Tanaka-like." Takemura continued: "Ideally, they should be a little more liberal, should carry out discussions more freely, and should be free from the bondage of the faction." These may be noble sentiments. But an Ozawa-imposed discipline may be precisely what is required to fill successfully the present power vacuum in Japanese politics.

There is also some reason to suspect the liberal creden-tials of Hosokawa himself. For he really stands for a form of bourgeois nationalism that has isolationist tendencies. This could sow the seeds for future conflict over the key issue of convergence with the far more internationalist-minded Ozawa. Takemura displayed similar tendencies in his *Chuo Koron* interview. Asked whether he agreed with a Hosokawa slogan that Japan should show its "unique being" to the world, Takemura concurred that he did. Yet anytime the word "unique" is used in the Japanese context it should set off alarm bells not only because it panders to the enduring ghosts of revisionism but also because it has ominous policy overtones on the whole issue of convergence.

Political philosophy aside, Hosokawa has also been shown to have undesirable political allies who in no way can be described as liberal. Press reports published in the summer of 1993 forced Hosokawa to admit publicly that in 1982 he had borrowed ¥100 million from Kiyoshi Sagawa, chairman of the by now notorious Sagawa Kyubin, to buy an apartment in Tokyo. Hosokawa also admitted he had received a total of ¥25 million in political contributions from Sagawa Kyubin over the previous six years, though he said he stopped receiving funds in the summer of 1991 by when the rumors about the pending scandal had begun to circulate in political circles. Another embarrassing link was that either Sagawa Kyubin or its Tokyo affiliate had rented out no fewer than three different Hosokawa residences at one time or another. The exposure of these links with Sagawa made Hosokowa, yet another former member of the Tanaka-Takeshita faction, look like just another venal politician.

Still, these revelations did not hurt Hosokawa's party in the summer elections. The Japan New Party was one of the few new alternatives, which the electorate craved to vote for. That is, so far as the voters craved anything, so alienated had they become from the political process. There was a record low turnout of 67 percent for the July general election despite the drama of the fall of Miyazawa's government. Its actual results proved almost an exact copy of the Tokyo election. The LDP's vote did not collapse, helped by the fact that the election was still fought under the old unreformed voting system, though the socialist vote did. But the LDP just failed to get the number of votes necessary to ensure their continued grip over government. A total of 230 seats would have given Miyazawa a hope of clinging to power, or at least such was his calculation prior to the election. In the event, the LDP only received 223 seats. The socialists got 70 seats (compared with

135 previously) and the Japan New Party and the Japan Renewal Party filled the resulting vacuum. Hosokawa's and Takemura's groups got a combined total of 48 seats and, impressively considering how little time it had had to prepare for the national poll, the Japan Renewal Party won 55 seats. This was a testimony to Ozawa's organizational and fund-raising skills.

The way was therefore paved for coalition government if Hosokawa and Ozawa could agree to work together. The man with the deciding vote was Hosokawa. After a week or so of prevarication, of flirting with one side, then the other, Hosokawa spurned the LDP and joined the opposition. His price, the deliberate result of his delaying tactics, was high: the prime ministership. He could demand it since his party represented the swing vote even though it was only the fourth largest in terms of votes in the seven-party coalition government. The coalition had 245 seats against the LDP's 225. Its membership was so disparate, from Hosokawa to Ozawa, from the socialists to the Komeito, a political spinoff from a religious sect, that it was hard to see a long life ahead for the new government. Its different members did agree though on one convenient policy slogan, political (i.e., electoral) reform. Yet within days of the Hosokawa government taking office it became clear that the new government would not be allowed the luxury of being able to concentrate in its first few months on reforming the electoral system and the related issue of political financing laws.

For the economy was weakening at such a pace, exacerbated by the soaring yen, that the bureaucratic and political establishment was being forced to admit what the business community had sensed for some time: that the Japanese economy was sliding into the uncharted territory of negative growth in direct contrast to official forecasts that still proclaimed recovery was at hand. This fact was confirmed with the release of the GNP figure for the three-month period from

April to June 1993, which showed the Japanese economy to be shrinking at an annualized rate of 2 percent. Such dramatic data suggested that the new government would likely be judged on how it managed the economy. Political reform was still important but in pragmatic Japan it would be viewed by the electorate as inconsequential compared with the social trauma posed by any surge in unemployment.

Significantly, in the formation of the Hosokawa cabinet all the important ministerial posts with regard to the management of the economy went to ex-Takeshita faction men who belonged to the Hata-Ozawa party. An example was MITI minister Kumagai, the same Kumagai who is quoted in the first chapter of this book arguing fervently about the need for deregulation. Kumagai soon reconfirmed his maverick tendencies when he stated on television following his appointment as MITI minister that there were structural reasons for Japan's trade surplus and that, if it was allowed to continue at its current size, it would be one factor leading to the destruction of the world economy. Strong stuff indeed. It showed that a key proponent of the need to deregulate the Japanese economy and promote consumption now occupied a position where he could do something about it. This was indeed a remarkable change.

Kumagai, like Ozawa, was on the correct track. Both men realized what many of Japan's senior and therefore most powerful mandarins still did not. This is that Japan only really faces one acceptable policy option to get out of its present economic problems without provoking a trade war (and that assumes the latest rise in the yen's value has not completely eroded the ability to export): stimulating domestic demand via the consumer, who also happens, conveniently, to vote. It is in this context that political realignment had become so necessary because as Andrew Ballingal, a Japanese investment strategist at British securities firm Barclays de Zoette Wedd, has written, "the old LDP and its attendant bureaucracy were still too obsessed with post-War nation building to allow any decadent consumerist notions to intrude into their saving/production/export-filled dreams."* Higher consumption would also have other benefits aside from boosting growth, such as higher imports and so hopefully a much better relationship with America.

But the other side of promoting consumption is the need to deregulate the domestic economy. This is required if consumers are to be allowed a genuine choice, which is why men like Kumagai recommend it. Indeed, deregulation became almost a vogue theme of the early weeks of the coalition government with vague promises being made of a bonfire of government decrees and regulations. Thus, claims were made by the new government that 10 percent of all regulations would be cut by April 1994. There are two problems with such admirable intentions. The first is that in the shorter term serious deregulation is bound to be extremely deflationary as price competition forces out weaker players, especially in those subsidized domestic industries that have long operated as not so informal cartels ripping off the consumer and that are as inefficient as Japan's great export companies used to be efficient. One example is the paper industry. Another is the commercial banking industry. This deflationary trend will be compounded if Japan is already suffering from an economy beset by excess production capacity, as indeed it now is. Jesper Koll, a Tokyo-based economist at British investment bank S. G. Warburg, described the problem well in a comment written shortly after the formation of the coalition government at a time when the deregulation fad was at its height: "Stepped up deregulation will eventually allow for efficiency increases, and hence improved profitability of the firms that survive the pick-up in competition implied in deregulation. The government's policy problem will be, however, to ensure

* "Silence of the Lambs," B2W Tokyo Research, June 26, 1993.

that deregulation does not unleash an uncontrollable deflationary spiral. At present, Japan's economy is suffering from excess capacity and excess employment [i.e., labor hoarding]. Breaking up a cartel under these sort of starting conditions triggers a tremendous downward adjustment to aggregate demand because of a sharp rise in unemployment."

Kumagai, the enthusiastic proponent of deregulation, had similar concerns in mind when he warned publicly in September that corporate restructuring and layoffs were inevitable and that Japan would undergo "painful times" for which there was "no quick panacea." This was indeed true given the economic trap that Japan was in. Yet it is far from certain that other parts of the political and bureaucratic establishment would agree that there is no choice, since Kumagai's comments assumed the market mechanism worked best. But the instinctive response of those resistant to convergence is likely to be the opposite of what is usually meant by deregulation. It could, for example, take the form of tapping taxpayers' money to preserve employment in industries that are no longer viable through employment subsidies and the like. The justification will be the need to prevent social conflict. Arguments over whether such policies are desirable will inevitably be a source of intense political conflict.

A key issue is therefore whether there is the necessary agreement within the coalition to implement real deregulation, and if there is whether there is sufficient political will to overcome an inevitably obstructionist bureaucracy. For all deregulation reduces the power of officialdom. Here the signs are not so optimistic. Buffeted by the weakening economy, the most important policy package announced in September 1993 by the new Hosokawa government was not electoral reform but rather yet another stimulatory economic package, the third since Japan's post-Bubble slowdown began in late 1990. It proved a big anticlimax. The ¥6.1 trillion stimulus was the usual array of public works spending and deliberate bureaucratic exaggeration in terms of the amount of extra oomph a certain amount of government spending will give to the economy. There was also a conspicuous lack of tax cuts, income or corporate, though a panel was set up to report on tax reform by April 1994. There was also some flirting with deregulation with a total of ninety-four deregulatory proposals. Some of these concentrated on making sure that consumers received the full benefit of the higher yen in terms of lower prices. This was fair enough considering the extent to which those handling imported goods in Japan have long unfairly profited at the expense of the consumer. Yet despite the ballyhoo made about such proposals the final effect in many cases was absurdly small. Thus, mandated cuts in electricity and gas rates implemented from November 1993 will provide average savings of ¥150 (or less than $1.50) per household per month. The total economic package, therefore, failed to inspire, with even Hosokawa admitting lamely at the time of its announcement that it would not be enough to revive the economy.

So the new government blew its chance to take control of economic policy. This was partly because its members could not agree among themselves but also because the bureaucrats remained powerful, and they were wary of radical reform of the tax system. Hosokawa, unlike Ozawa, is not the man to take on the Finance Ministry. These battles will therefore be left to be fought another day, and fought they will be. For yet another economic package has now become inevitable and the longer the economy fails to recover, the greater the likelihood that ambitious politicians will take on the bureaucracy itself, and in particular the Finance Ministry. That raises the potential for populist tax-cutting politics in Japan with the venerated bureaucracy cast as villains. For the point is that Japanese politics is no longer stable. The Hosokawa-led coalition will break apart once political reform, on which all coalition members agree, is out of the way. For friction over economic policy will escalate as the unholy combination of a high yen and excess production capacity takes its cruel toll on the industrial base and the once sacred employment system. Rising numbers of jobless in Japan will inevitably raise the convergence issue within the Japanese political system, since it will make brutally clear the policy choices that Japan as a country will have to decide on. That is whether to go the Anglo-Saxon free market way, a way most of the rest of the world is now eagerly copying, or to opt for a panoply of controls and subsidies in the aim of defending the status quo whatever the cost in terms of subsidizing inefficiency. The former approach will seem dangerously destabilizing at the time but it will ultimately result in a much stronger and more competitive Japan, just as American business has become massively more competitive as a result of the past five years of almost constant restructuring. It should always be remembered that the market's ruthless purging of losers creates opportunities for newcomers. A would-be entrepreneur can set up a new business that much more cheaply if he can buy a manufacturing plant or warehouse out of receivership from a company that has been allowed to go bankrupt. In America that marking-to-market process is part of everyday life. In Japan it too often is not. This failure to let prices clear is now undermining the ability of the economy to recover.

If Japan fails this test and opts to use the still huge savings in its private sector to subsidize the inefficient, this fast-aging country will be destined to experience at best slow but steady ossification. Genteel decline is what another island, once blessed with a commercial empire, has experienced for the past century (though admittedly the process was accelerated in the noble cause of financing the fight against the Nazis in the Second World War). Yet Japan does not have to suffer Britain's ultimately dreary fate. But for that destiny to be avoided the country is going to have to produce some statesmen capable of both articulating the challenges facing the country and forging a new consensus on the goals to pursue. For the bureaucrats will continue only to defend their own turf, sure in their view that they are the only true guardians of the national interest.

This is why Japanese politics has suddenly become so important. The Hosokawa-led coalition is clearly only the first step in Japan's political realignment, though a necessary one since it has brought about the end of continuous LDP government. It is the hors d'oeuvre in what could turn out to be a long banquet. For there are clear choices that have to be made before a new consensus can be formed, be they over economic policy, foreign policy or indeed the continued relevance of the postwar constitution itself. And all relate back to the key issue of convergence.

Japan clearly works best as a society when there is an agreed consensus. But sometimes a consensus is not possible. This is the new reality that now faces Japan. The last great consensus has now broken down after nearly fifty years of almost constant success in terms of economic growth and material rises in the Japanese people's standard of living. It has broken down because of the many problems that will be described in this book. The new consensus has yet to take shape. However, the less fragmented Japanese politics now becomes, the quicker such a new consensus will be formed; the messier the politics, the longer will be the period of debilitating conflict. Former newspaper editor Utagawa raises in his paper three possible ways for Japanese politics to develop. The first and the healthiest would be a two-party system born out of the old LDP with genuine policy debate and an electorate offered a real alternative. This would represent a mature Japanese democracy. Japan would enjoy the substance of parliamentary democracy as opposed to merely its form, which has been the case until now. The second possibility is a multitude of parties spawning governments of shifting coalitions. This sort of Italian experience is clearly unstable. A third possibility is a form of grand coalition including virtually all parties and based on lowest common policy denominators on which all can agree. This is also not desirable, since it is likely to be a recipe for weak policy and a continued lack of decision making. The Hosokawa-led coalition reveals some of these unsettling tendencies.

The hope and likelihood is that Japan will develop the desired two-party system, since it is not a nation that either appreciates or indeed tolerates prolonged instability. The Japanese revere order. They are therefore likely to develop a political system that produces it in one way or another. The hope must be that Japan will rise to the very real challenges posed by the financial collapse of the bursting of the Bubble and the subsequent downturn in the real economy, and that the country will emerge out of this traumatic period with a political system that will reflect the needs and aspirations of what is a predominantly affluent and urban late-twentieth-century society. But whether this process proves smooth or chaotic will depend primarily on the future course of the economy.

3

The Economy—
No Quick Fix

INCREDIBLY, the self-denial continued for so long. On June 10, 1993, Hajime Funada, then head of the official Economic Planning Agency (EPA), told the Japanese cabinet he was "sure the economy has hit bottom"—just as his predecessor had done the previous year. But this time the EPA chief did not go the whole hog. He refrained from formally declaring the recession over, as he had originally wanted to. He was forced to retreat from this absurdly confident stance by cabinet dissension. But even this qualified endorsement of economic recovery drew widespread guffaws in most quarters, including from some other government ministries. Yoshiro Mori, then minister for international trade and industry, told a press conference the next day that the EPA should realize by now that this was "no normal cyclical downturn" and that the usual indicators of recovery might not prove so reliable.

This comment was completely to the point. As the politician with responsibility for MITI, whose officials are closest to the problems now confronting corporate Japan, Mori had a firmer grasp on reality. For most of the main economic policy makers in the Japanese government, be they at the EPA, the Ministry of Finance or the Bank of Japan, have been consistently and spectacularly wrong during the past three years in their persistently premature forecasts of economic recovery. As a result, they have lost a huge amount of credibility, especially with the business community whom they have continuously misled with their rosy forecasts. These officials have also demonstrated a profound lack of imagination in the way they have tried to counter what is without doubt the biggest economic crisis Japan has faced since the Second World War. Unfortunately, the combination of inept forecasting and an inadequate policy response ensures that the economic problems will persist for far longer than most conventional economists even now still think.

Officialdom's failure is not surprising, since most of the key government policy makers have continued for far too long to regard this recession, which began in early 1991, as a normal cyclical adjustment. Their response has therefore been singularly conventional. Two major fiscal expansions in September 1992 and March 1993, worth collectively ¥23.9 trillion in terms of the headline figures announced, have sought to pump demand into the economy primarily by boosting public works spending. Such fiscal stimulus, however, has only succeeded in preventing the economy from entering into an outright free fall. Growth will at best remain marginal until the middle of this decade. That this is not a normal Japanese-style recession is already clear. Japan's GNP shrank at an annualized rate of 2 percent in the second quarter of 1993 following several consecutive quarters that had registered a declining growth rate. So, far from recovering, the recession is actually getting worse. The economy has been suffering from a vicious cycle of corporate retrenchment and consumer caution. The only factor that has so far prevented GNP growth from turning outrightly negative for a whole year, aside from public works spending, has been a positive contribution from the trade balance. Japan's current account surplus has continued to soar, with all the alarming prospects for trade friction that this development portends. The trade surplus reached $120 billion in 1993 and the bilateral surplus with America totaled $50 billion. Yet this time the soaring trade surplus has been less a function of rising exports than of a collapse in the demand for imports, which is itself a reflection of the weakness of domestic demand.

Japan is therefore in the midst of a painful hangover from the euphoric Bubble years. But the current slump is far more than the natural reaction to cyclical speculative excesses that the government and its propagandists in the private sector and the press have sought to portray it as. Proponents of this complacently optimistic view fail to comprehend that the Japanese economy is undergoing two profound adjustments that are both structural and secular in nature. The first is admittedly now better understood than the second and was the subject of the author's previous books.* It is the natural reaction to the late 1980s credit boom. For the bursting of the Bubble Economy has indeed proved not to have been confined only to those sectors most caught up in the speculation, namely finance and property, but has impacted the real economy. Japan is now suffering from a full-scale debt deflation that could yet turn into outright deflation in terms of a general fall in the price level. Its symptoms are familiar since they have been visible in many countries during the late 1980s and early 1990s. It is a world of financial stress, of weak if not shrinking money and credit growth, of falling property values and rising bankruptcies. It is a world where companies slash business investment and where consumers turn increasingly cautious both because their main asset (property) has fallen in value and because their main source of cash flow (their job) is increasingly perceived to be at risk.

The second adjustment facing Japan, however, is less

* Boom and Bust: The Rise and Fall of World Financial Markets (Atheneum, 1989) and The Bubble Economy (The Atlantic Monthly Press, 1992).

recognized but far more important in the longer term. This is the belated response by Japanese business to the recognition that Japan's long-term sustainable economic growth rate is now probably only 3 percent at best. This new reality has dramatic implications. It means radical changes in the employment system. Lifetime employment and the seniority system, the pillars of a salaried man's life in the larger companies, are no longer assured. In fact they are doomed. For labor costs can no longer go on being allowed to rise unchecked. This means changes in the way companies manage themselves and how they plan ahead. Company managers will in future be required to concentrate on improving the return on capital invested. This will be considered of far more importance than such traditional obsessions as turnover and market share.

The new reality will mean a dramatic one-off decline in domestic capital spending, marking a profound shift from Japan's post-1945 model of economic development, which was based on heavy business investment and the export-driven pursuit of market share in world markets. This transition process has only just begun. It is likely to continue until at least the middle of this decade, since Japanese industry is glutted with excess production capacity in high-cost Japan. Since capital spending peaked at 22 percent of the GNP in 1991 the Japanese economy will remain weak at best during this traumatic adjustment period.

Smithers & Co., a London-based investment research boutique, published in May 1993 a paper that focused on the secular nature of the current decline in Japanese business investment.* It describes this process as the natural consequence of what is called appropriately Japan's "other bubble." This bubble was not the speculative boom in the stock market and property market but a massive capital-spending binge by Japanese business driven by the then availability of super-

* *"Japan's Other Bubble: The Causes and Consequences of the Secular Trend of Corporate Investment,"* May 1993.

cheap finance and the conviction on the part of most companies that a demographic-inspired and much feared labor shortage justified the need to spend large sums of money on automation and other labor-saving devices. In fact, the labor shortage during the late 1980s was actually less severe than in 1972–1973 when the job to offer ratio rose to a peak of 1.9. Yet capital spending as a share of total economic output was far greater in this later period. For corporate Japan overinvested on a heroic scale. Capital spending accounted for two thirds of GNP growth between late 1986 and early 1981, the duration of the so-called *Heisei* expansion. This investment frenzy made no sense. For corporate Japan was increasing the productive capacity of the domestic economy during this period at a rate which suggested that its businessmen thought Japan was still a developing economy in the midst of a transformation to becoming an industrial economy, and one that did not face any political constraints on further expanding its trade surplus. Both premises were false. Japan is an aging society, many of whose domestic markets are mature, and whose future growth rates will look far more like America's or the countries of Western Europe than its Asian neighbors. Meanwhile the patience of Japan's trading partners has long since been exhausted as regards the persistent trade surplus. As a result, much of the investment undertaken by business in recent years will never earn an adequate rate of return. Indeed, it is the unprofitability of all this domestic capital spending, rather than excess production capacity per se, that is now the central problem facing Japanese industry and the economy in general. The shocking because unexpected 20 percent-plus rise in the value of the yen in the first half of 1993 has only compounded this problem for Japan's exporters by raising that much higher the cost of producing in Japan. It has also exposed domestic companies to the shock of cheap imports at a time when the Japanese consumer has suddenly turned price conscious.

The difficulties that Japan has encountered in trying to maintain its traditionally high level of domestic investment are clear from the country's deteriorating capital to output ratio. It takes more and more investment to deliver a given increase in output. This means that a steady growth in national income can only be sustained by a steadily rising proportion of national income being devoted to investment. Such a development is unstable since, put another way, stable growth requires not only an accelerating rate of investment but also a steady decline in the proportion of the GNP consumed. This trend has therefore resulted in an increasingly lopsided form of economic activity. The Bubble years marked this trend taken to its logical though absurd extreme. Paul Summerville, a Tokyo-based economist at American investment bank Lehman Brothers, has captured this trend graphically. He describes Japan's economy in 1990 as the "elephant-man economy" as a result of the distortions posed by a mature economy devoting such a large amount of economic output to capital investment. And it is large by the standards of the developed economies. As a proportion of national income, investment, and its counterpart savings, are one and a half times the level found in France, Italy and Germany and twice those found in America and Britain. It is this distortion that is about to be corrected in a manner that will mark the end of Japan's post-1945 model of economic development.

Japan's deteriorating capital to output ratio has its counterpart in the country's declining long-term trend-growth rate. It also is a process that, though widely ignored by most conventional economists, has been going on for some time. Japan's annual trend-growth rate in real GNP in the decade leading up to the first OPEC oil shock was 8.8 percent. Since 1975 it has declined to 4.25 percent, though perversely the key ratio of capital investment to GNP was higher in the second period than in the first. As a result, there has been a sharp decline in the return on capital invested. Business investment became even more unprofitable in the most recent capital spending binge during the Bubble years. However, looking forward Japan can in the future expect a trend in real GNP growth of only 3 percent at best—2.5 percent is probably a more realistic estimate. This means that at the depth of the business cycle the economy is likely to contract as it does regularly in America or Europe. Officially the government still hopes for a 4 percent long-term growth rate. In private, officials increasingly tend to be much more conservative. Japan, land of the economic miracle, is destined to face Anglo-Saxon growth rates.

There are several reasons for this significant slowdown in Japan's ability to grow. First, from the 1990s on it is unrealistic to expect productivity growth to be boosted by employment growth. Population growth is now close to zero, as is the growth rate of the working-age population, the consequence of the fact that the average reproduction rate of a Japanese woman is now only 1.5. Japan's labor force will on present demographic trends actually begin to decline in the year 2001. Second, women's participation in the labor force probably peaked at 60 percent in the late 1980s. Women are now invariably and cruelly among the first to be laid off in the present hard times because they are usually not part of the formal lifetime employment system. Third, working hours are likely to fall substantially as part of the official effort to improve the "quality" of life. The net result is that real GNP growth will depend almost entirely on productivity growth, which is unlikely to exceed the 3 percent average annual growth rate in productivity recorded during the 1970s and 1980s.

This means that a further substantial decline in business investment lies ahead on top of the retrenchment already announced as businessmen respond to the more subdued growth outlook. For American and European experience suggests that an appropriate ratio for capital spending to GNP in a mature economy is about 12 percent. In Japan that ratio peaked at 22 percent in 1991. It is worth noting that capital spending reached a similarly high percentage of America's GNP in late 1920s America prior to the Great Depression. Most Japanese companies have since 1991 announced steep reductions in planned investment, but capital spending still accounted for 20.5 percent of the GNP in 1992. Therefore, further massive cutbacks seem inevitable with all the unpleasant consequences that implies both for the employment system and consumer confidence. It is quite reasonable to expect capital spending in Japan to decline by almost one half before this adjustment process is completed until it accounts for just 12 percent of GNP. Many will regard this prediction as far too alarmist. But it would be unwise to underestimate companies' readiness to react once they are convinced that growth prospects are not as glowing as they once assumed. Indeed, Japan's historical experience suggests that a downward trend in capital spending to GNP once begun tends to last for at least four years. This was indeed the case after the first oil shock and it will be so again.

Corporate Japan also has another factor to consider beyond the long-term growth prospects or rather the lack of them. That is excess production capacity. This may not be the central problem. But it is still a substantial one. Many major industries, such as autos, still have far too much domestic manufacturing capacity. Further decisions to mothball capacity, such as Nissan's decision in early 1992 to close its Zama plant outside Tokyo, can be confidently expected. This will form part of an already clear longer-term trend often fashionably referred to as the "hollowing out" of Japan, where more and more Japanese manufacturing will be located offshore, particularly in lower-cost Asia. It will not be long, for example, before video recorders are no longer made in Japan. But it will not just be exporters who will be shifting production overseas. So will long-protected inefficient domestic industries like paper, cement and rubber who have been saved from import competition by cartel-like arrangements. They have kept in business by selling their products to Japanese consumers at very high prices. But that strategy has now reached such ludicrous extremes, with the latest jump in the yen, that it has become both unsustainable and indefensible in an increasingly consumer-conscious society. One cement company in mid-1993 was selling cement on the domestic market at ¥10,750 per ton but exporting it for only ¥3,500 per ton.

So far the manufacturing sector has led the way in announcing cuts in domestic capital spending. Toyota, for example, at the parent company level announced it would cut its investment budget from a peak of ¥600 billion in the fiscal year that ended in March 1992 to a planned ¥300 billion in the year to March 1995. However, the manufacturing sector only accounted for 36 percent of business investment in 1992. The nonmanufacturing sector, which comprises the rest, has been slower to wake up to the new harsh realities mainly because the economic slowdown only really hit the service sector in the second half of 1992. Service companies have also now begun to cut, though, and will continue to do so with growing vigor. Most vulnerable are the numerous nonmanufacturing subsidiaries that manufacturing firms set up in the late 1980s, such as hair dressers, travel agencies, restaurants, software companies and even wedding agencies. These subsidiaries were established less to make money than to absorb excess employees. Many of them will now close or at least suffer death by a thousand cuts.

This crunch in the service sector also has implications that extend beyond the area of capital spending into employment. For the service sector has now gone into recession for the first time since the launching of the economic miracle. MITI's index of tertiary sector output, which is the best measure of the Japanese service sector available, declined by 0.5 percent between October and December 1992. This development means that the impact of the present recession on employment will eventually be far worse than in the first OPEC oil shock. Between 1973 and 1975, 1.8 million jobs were lost in manufacturing, mostly in heavy industry. But this shrinkage was largely offset by a still-growing service sector. That will not happen this time since the service sector job engine is now running out of steam. It already accounts for 50 percent of total employment compared with 44 percent in 1980.

An added complication is the nature of the industries that will have to be restructured. In the 1970s this process was managed under bureaucratic guidance. MITI labeled the steel or shipbuilding industries, for example, as "structurally depressed" industries and formulated an equitable pain-sharing plan whereby each producer cut a preagreed amount of its production capacity. The intervention of the central government also meant that the dismissing of employees could be depicted as part of a centrally organized national strategy, a collective sharing of pain. Even better, as part of this corporatist deal, prices were usually fixed. So, face was saved, retraining for the discarded was arranged, the taxpayer funded the resulting "employment-adjustment subsidies" and the consumer was, as usual, the loser.

This sort of traditional approach, however, will be far harder if not impossible to implement with the two manufacturing industries most painfully affected by the current recession. These are autos and electronics, the two star export sectors that made the Japanese economic miracle possible, and their respective chains of components suppliers. These two industries have never been under heavy MITI influence, which is probably why they have for the most part been so successful. It should be noted that MITI's role in creating the Japanese miracle has been hugely exaggerated by conspiracy-obsessed Western believers in the all-embracing powers of Japan Inc. The ministry ceased to have much influence on the economy at least twenty years ago since when perhaps its main function has been to organize bailouts of depressed domestic industries. Even when MITI's power was at its peak in the 1950s and 1960s, on account of its role in allocating precious foreign exchange among sectors, the ministry's "guidance" was not always so helpful. The carmakers regularly resisted MITI's interventionist efforts to order a top-down rationalization of the industry. Honda and Sony are perhaps the two most famous examples of post-1945 Japanese corporate success stories that prospered despite MITI, not because of it. Hence the famous story of MITI nearly putting Sony out of business in 1948 when it refused that then small company's request for some foreign exchange to buy transistor manufacturing rights from Western Electric.

It is obvious that today Toyota would fiercely resist any attempt by MITI to impose on it a pain-sharing bureaucratic-led restructuring of the car industry. As the dominant producer with by far the biggest market share as well as the strongest balance sheet it is simply not in Toyota's interest to conform to such a plan. Rather, it will want to exploit market forces to use the current distress to further strengthen its own position. There is also another factor. Foreign governments would be most likely to resist any overt attempt by the Japanese government to bail out its carmakers at a time when they have such a large share of world export markets.

Yet the auto and electronics industries have to retrench, as will be discussed in detail in later chapters. For they, like most of the rest of corporate Japan, need to undergo a fundamental restructuring. This is what many American companies have already gone through in recent years. The result has been much pain but also a considerable increase in competitiveness; a trend known as jobless prosperity. Since 1989 when the American economic slowdown first became evident, American companies have shed more than 7 million jobs in a process that has been given the ugly name "downsizing."

And, unusually, the job losses have fallen equally between the white-collar and the blue-collar sectors. This has therefore been a middle-class recession. Suburban dormitory towns in America are now filled in the daytime with middle-aged former executives caught in a trap of enforced idleness, a pattern that if repeated in Japan will cause social chaos.

This restructuring frenzy is why American companies earnings have risen, and the New York stock market has rallied to new all-time highs, despite the continuing absence of a convincing rebound in final demand. The pain in human terms has been considerable but the benefits in terms of productivity have been enormous since so many of the jobs destroyed had become redundant with the advent of information technology. This new competitive reality posed by a recharged corporate America, coupled with the ever present threat of protectionism, is the challenge that now faces Japanese businessmen. It is a daunting one. Their practical problem is that as a result of the late 1980s capital-spending spree, key industrial sectors of the Japanese economy have installed more productive capacity than they need for many years ahead. Yet so far the pain resulting from this excess has only been reflected in companies' accounts. Japanese firms reported for the first time since 1945 their third consecutive year of declining profits in the financial year that ended in March 1993, the consequence primarily of all that investment, which has raised firms' break-even points in terms of the amount of goods they have to sell to make a profit. So, earnings have slumped as a result of stagnant sales, soaring depreciation charges to pay for all that investment, and (for exporters) a rising yen. In this sense the latest surge in the yen in 1993 to near the symbolic 100 level has come at the worst possible time.

Businessmen are naturally complaining loudly. But the bureaucrats, as usual, are too complacent. They argue that the rise in the yen is so far nowhere near as steep as the near doubling in value that occurred following the 1985 Plaza Accord, the international agreement to reduce the value of the dollar by central bank intervention. But comparisons with the post-Plaza period may not be so relevant. First, the yen may have appreciated by a far smaller percentage so far. But the rally has begun from a far higher base level. Most exporters are unprofitable at a rate of ¥115 or higher. Worse, many Japanese companies have not hedged themselves against a rising yen since they did not expect it to appreciate against the dollar beyond the ¥120 level given the weakness of the domestic economy. Second, since corporate profits are already so depressed, companies have less room for maneuver to withstand the impact of a rising yen. In 1985 the profits of the car and electronics industries amounted to about 6 percent of their sales. Now profits are only around 1 percent of sales and falling, since profits in these two sectors will have declined for the fourth year in a row in the fiscal year that ended in March 1994. Worse, in the car industry especially, American producers have become more competitive in terms of the products they sell. Consequently, Japanese carmakers are now losing market share in America as they are forced by the appreciating yen to raise prices. The rising yen also has its dark side for purely domestic companies. The last time the yen rallied post-Plaza, importers pocketed the windfall and the consumer did not benefit. This has not happened on this occasion. There is now growing price competition from imported goods in Japan, be the product clothing, consumer durables, processed foods, computers or even cars. The Japanese subsidiary of Britain's Rover, for example, cut the price of its cars by an average of 13 percent in February 1993. Its sales rose by 33 percent in the first four months of the same year despite a depressed local car market. For the weakness of the domestic economy has meant that for the first time in recent memory the Japanese consumer has become price conscious. As a consequence, discounting is now rampant in the retail industry, which is another aspect of Japan's new reality. This may be good for the consumer but it is bad for profits. The result is that the latest surge in the yen will mean a fourth consecutive year of declining earnings for corporate Japan as a whole. Yet profits are already at very depressed levels. Companies' pretax earnings are likely to have declined to at least as low as 3 percent of GNP in the financial year that ended March 1994, which is where they troughed at the end of 1974.

Certainly, the longer radical restructuring is delayed the greater will be the slump in corporate profitability. As practical men of commerce Japanese businessmen know what it means to be uncompetitive. They also increasingly realize what they have to do to restore their competitiveness, since the diminished long-term growth prospects make it extremely unlikely that they can just grow their way out of their problems. Retrenchment is required. Companies have to cut their fixed costs. Their problem is how to go about it, for their biggest fixed cost is personnel. Japanese manufacturing companies' unit labor costs have soared since early 1991, in part because of rising labor costs and in part because of falling production. By contrast, American manufacturers' unit labor costs have hardly risen since the slowdown began in 1989, a function of aggressive cost controls and a realistic assessment of the lackluster condition of the economy. This development threatens Japan's famous lifetime employment system, and indeed the very basis of Japanese-style capitalism, which is supposed according to Sakakibara to put employees before shareholders. The world is about to find out if, when it comes to the crunch, Japanese capitalism is really so different after all.

It was certainly clear that Japanese businessmen, at least in private, were by the middle of 1993 increasingly prepared to admit that the system of lifetime employment as applied in larger companies was no longer a viable one in the longer term, given both Japan's reduced growth prospects and its growing lack of competitiveness. They were also waking up to the fact that, after years of swallowing government propaganda about a supposedly acute labor shortage, they were in reality employing too many people.

Ken Nagano, chairman of the Japan Federation of Employers Association (Nikkeiren), set the tone in the 1993 *shunto* annual wage negotiations between employers and trade unions by stating flatly that falling profits and "underemployment" meant that wages should only be increased by 2.3 percent in 1993. Nagano also stated that workers should not expect any increases in either overtime or bonuses for that year. Furthermore, the Nikkeiren leader went yet one more stage. He actually sought to define the level of underemployment. Nagano stated that Japanese companies employ 1.2 million excess workers, an amount equivalent to 2 percent of the total workforce. If they all lost their jobs, that would double at one stroke Japan's official unemployment rate from 2.5 percent to 5 percent.

The fact of overstaffing has also now been acknowledged, albeit tacitly, by the government, in a sign that belief in a structural labor shortage is no longer official policy. A survey by the Ministry of Labor published in early 1993 found, not so surprisingly, that several industries reported they were overstaffed. In fact, the degree of overmanning is even higher than the Nikkeiren's estimate. Peter Morgan, an economist at Merrill Lynch in Tokyo, calculated in early 1993 that there were at least 2 million excess workers in Japan, an amount equivalent to 3 percent of total employment. The main reason for this excess is that Japanese companies kept on hiring at a brisk pace between 1989 and 1991 because they believed in a labor shortage despite growing signs of an economic slowdown. Morgan describes this process as a "speculative hoarding of labor." This situation is even pronounced in the manufacturing sector where companies continued to hire despite an

absolute decline in output. Manufacturing employment between June and November 1992, for example, rose by 1 percent year-on-year. Yet industrial production during the same
period declined by 6 percent year-on-year. Morgan estimated
that there are 1.3 million excess workers in the manufacturing
sector alone based on this discrepancy between employment
growth and output growth since 1989. This would mean only
700,000 excess workers for the rest of the economy. Since the
manufacturing sector accounts for only 24 percent of all employment in Japan, even a 2 million underemployed figure
looks very much on the low side. A total of 3 million is probably more realistic.

The employment system is therefore ripe for radical adjustment, a development that is fraught with huge social and
political as well as economic consequences. And as in America
the area most in need of pruning is the white-collar category.
About three quarters of the 7 million additions to the Japanese labor force hired between 1987 and 1991 were white-
collar workers. Even in the manufacturing sector more than
half the existing labor force now comprises white-collar staff.
So any serious restructuring will have to address this area,
especially as these workers are far less productive. They also
on account of the seniority system tend to be far more expensive. A Nikkeiren report published in late 1991 actually con-
trasts the improved productivity of blue-collar workers with
the declining productivity of their white-collar colleagues.

Still, Japanese companies have lots of room to maneuver
if they choose to bite the bullet. A total of 21 percent of the
Japanese workforce is above the early retirement age of sixty-
five. So they can in theory be shed with little pain, thereby
reaping substantial savings. Baring Securities has estimated
that the total wage and salary bill of the 1,600 Japanese companies (excluding financial firms) listed on Japan's Topix stock
market index, the equivalent of America's Standard & Poor's
500, was more than ¥28 trillion in the fiscal year that ended

March 1992 while their total pretax profits that same year were just over ¥10 trillion. Assuming very crudely that these employees' age profile is similar to the national average and that each employee receives the average wage regardless of age, then if the 4.33 million workers aged over fifty-five retired early the wage bill would be cut by some ¥1.8 trillion. This is equivalent to 18 percent of these companies' pretax profits in the financial year that ended in March 1992 and a higher percentage of their reduced earnings to March 1993.

Such are the potential benefits of cost cutting. The problem for major Japanese companies, however, is how to secure these savings in a socially acceptable way. For the reality is that it is very hard to do so, especially as the government has continued to provide no lead. Its official policy continues to be that such a radical adjustment in the employment system is not only unnecessary but also positively dangerous. This is forcing companies to adopt lots of indirect ways of cutting costs, many of which may in the longer term prove counterproductive. The bureaucracy's stance remains clear. Outright sackings by established companies are not acceptable. The Labor Ministry, for example, in February 1993 publicly called on employers not to shed labor. Kunihiko Saito, head of the ministry's employment security bureau, even counseled against early retirement and the reduction of the number of graduates hired, both increasingly popular ploys of employers seeking to cut costs. The official said that such measures would create great worries over employment prospects throughout society and "undermine the social trust in companies." Later the same month Funada of the EPA went a step further. He urged companies to boost salaries to bolster consumer confidence. This harebrained advice was bound to be ignored since businessmen were by then well aware of the need to retrench. Yet Funada's comment, however silly, was revealing. It showed that the bureaucrats were not only concerned about defending the traditional employment system. They were also increasingly worried about the impact of the growing fear of unemployment on the level of consumption. The Labor Ministry added to the pressure on companies by threatening to publish a list of offending companies that had unilaterally revoked agreements to hire graduates.

But as they sought to humiliate in public the naughty boys of the corporate sector the government remained completely silent about how Japanese companies could otherwise get their costs under control. This made the bureaucrats look at best detached, at worst plain foolish. Faced with this vacuum at the top, businessmen will increasingly be forced to take matters into their own hands. The enduring complacency of the political establishment toward this whole question was reflected in comments made by Seizaburo Sato in an interview in May 1993. Sato is the executive director at the Institute for International Policy Studies, a think tank founded by former prime minister Yasuhiro Nakasone and staffed by mid-level bureaucrats and large-company executives. Sato is a political scientist rather than an economist. But as Nakasone's former national security adviser and a well-known face on the international conference circuit he is probably the nearest thing there is to a Henry Kissinger in Japan; a member of the great and the good and certainly a pillar of Japan's political establishment. The complacency of his views on the economy was therefore noteworthy. They reflected the opinion of much of the bureaucracy that any corporate restructuring need not be so dramatic. Confident that the Japanese economy was about to pick up strongly, Sato noted that businessmen always exaggerate their problems in recessions, adding that any efforts to get rid of supposedly excess labor would be catastrophic. "If Japanese managers followed the American example that would be a disaster. If you fire the employees there would be a serious demoralization of the work ethic." This is an interesting comment since it highlights a fundamental difference in attitude. In the West if a person is fired it raises the incentive to work harder. But in Japan dismissals would only demoralize the workforce since it would be such a clear flouting of the social contract. Here again is expressed the view that Japanese companies exist for the employee not the shareholder. Yet Sato has no proposals to offer Japanese firms about how to get out of their predicament if only because he does not understand that they are in one. This amounts to a total failure to comprehend, let alone acknowledge, Japan's dramatic loss of competitiveness.

Those companies that have thus far tried to adopt a more aggressive approach have encountered public opprobrium. Such was the response when in January 1993 the Japanese press reported that Pioneer, an audio equipment maker, had told thirty-five senior employees aged fifty and over that they had to leave the company. In most countries this sort of compulsory early retirement would not be considered such a big deal provided the severance terms were fair. Not so in Japan where it was taken as a signal that the famed lifetime employment system was indeed breaking down under the pressure of recession. Japanese capitalism had suddenly become less victimless. The terms were that Pioneer would offer the thirty-five employees up to two years' compensation provided they agreed to leave the company by the end of January. If any declined they would continue to be persuaded to leave, though Pioneer stressed somewhat lamely in response to a barrage of press questions that an agreement would be reached by "mutual understanding," not by outright dismissal. Katsuhiro Abe, general manager of Pioneer's personnel division, said in an interview at the time that the decision was taken less to save money—the thirty-five employees only cost the company in terms of salary and bonus about ¥10 million each—than to set an example to the firm's nine thousand employees in Japan to demonstrate the need to work harder in tough times. This approach would perhaps have had a better chance of succeeding if Pioneer had been more straightforward about delivering its message. But sadly for company morale, and perhaps for its future ability to recruit the best graduates, shocked Pioneer employees learned about the proposed dismissals in their newspapers rather than through an internal circular. Still, the company's reasoning in many ways made a lot of sense. The thirty-five who were asked to leave had no subordinates working under them and belonged to the category of Japanese salaried men known as *madogiwa-zoku*. This is the derogatory expression used to describe employees who spend the final years of their career literally gazing out the window. Abe said that by leaving, these men would be able to enjoy a second productive career working for a small- or medium-sized firm that would value their experience at a major company even though the salary paid would probably be about 20 percent lower. That is certainly more productive an arrangement, and arguably also a more humane one, than an existence of idly waiting for retirement ignored and also probably scorned by colleagues. Yet despite the comparative modesty of its proposed retrenchment, following a wave of adverse publicity Pioneer was forced to back down from its plan about a month after it was first leaked in the press. The company's official line was that it was reconsidering its position. This was taken by some as a sign of the strength of the Japanese system; that lifetime employment would never change. The real message, however, was bearish. The long overdue change would only be deferred. Japanese companies would take longer to react to their eroding profitability and therefore longer to restore their competitiveness.

For with outright dismissals of full-time male employees still not considered socially acceptable for major companies, employers have had to use every other expedient available to them to cut personnel costs. There are several such ways, most of which are not really satisfactory, and all of them are being resorted to. They include the following. First, part-time and seasonal workers who are not members of the company union can be laid off immediately. These two categories tend to include foreign workers and women, both of whom are not part of the traditional lifetime employment system. They also do not appear in the unemployment statistics. Second, employees are posted to subsidiaries. This can mean a move to a nonjob and even to a desk without a telephone. In the cruel and unforgiving world that can be Japan's labor market such a transfer can also be the kiss of death financially as well as emotionally. For the employee is usually put on a different contract, which invariably means he is paid less. He can also subsequently be fired more easily because he is no longer a member of the company union. However, such transfers are increasingly hard to push through since it has become difficult to find profitable subsidiaries willing and able to warehouse these excess employees. This has resulted in a third approach. Transferring employees to customers or suppliers, or even competitors, as it has become harder to find suppliers or clients willing to take on surplus labor. Thus it was announced in February 1993 that Sega Enterprises, the then fast-growing video game company and chief rival of Nintendo, had hired sixteen managers on a temporary basis from six major electronics companies outside its own keiretsu* group. The companies were Hitachi, Fujitsu, NEC, Oki Electronics, Toshiba and Fuji. The deal in what began as a one-year arrangement was that Sega would bear only a part of the managers' costs. This was a twist from the normal practice of Japanese companies dumping surplus staff onto group companies or subsidiaries. However, Sega is unusual among Japanese companies in that its sales and profits were still growing. The company was therefore happy to pick up management on the cheap from companies with whom it already has a business relationship since it buys semiconductors from them.

* A keiretsu is a group of companies linked by cross-share holdings, such as the Mitsubishi or the Mitsui groups.

But there are not many companies in Japan at the moment in so fortunate a position outside certain flourishing niche areas, of which video games is one and discount retailing is another.

Other forms of corporate retrenchment resorted to could probably only occur in Japan. They include paying bonuses in kind in the form of the companies' own product, for example consumer electronics items, and ordering workers on full pay to stay at home. Such practices highlight the extraordinary lengths companies will go to avoid layoffs. Another increasingly favored option is sharply reducing the number of graduates hired even to the extent of revoking previous commitments to take on graduate students. A *Nikkei Keizei Shimbun* survey of 1,200 companies found they cut their graduate intake by 21 percent in the financial year that ended in March 1993 and planned a similar cut for the following year. This is clearly not the wisest form of long-term planning, since today's graduate trainee represents tomorrow's senior management. Also, graduate trainees are hardly the highest-cost labor. Yet students who have just graduated are viewed as expendable since they are not yet part of the employment system.

Such a rigid way of thinking is not the way to sustain Japan's competitiveness in a world of bewildering technological change and massive downward pressure on wage costs as countries outside the ranks of the Organization of Economic Cooperation and Development forsake (in the case of Eastern Europe and China) Soviet planning models or (in the case of Latin America or India) import-substitution models, and start to compete as capitalists, taking on in the process the high-cost producers. In such a world inflexibly rigid high-cost employment systems are a massive liability, a reality that has become painfully apparent not only in Japan but also in that other stubborn adherent to an outmoded corporatist model, Germany.

With all this uncertainty on the employment front it is

not surprising that consumption has weakened in Japan to a far greater extent than the government and most private economists ever expected it to. The reason is that economists track theoretical econometric models based on post-1945 economic data, whereas the consumer reacts psychologically to what he or she senses around him. Since at least early 1992 the average salaried man has got the message from his company that times are tough. That message would have been duly passed on to his wife, who controls the purse strings in most Japanese households. The result is that it has not needed a steep rise in unemployment to cause the consumer to take fright. Private consumer spending slowed in real terms to a rise of just 0.3 percent year-on-year in the last three months of 1992. This unexpected parsimony reflected dwindling income growth, flat bonuses and the sharply reduced number of overtime hours worked. Bonuses and overtime are key since they account for up to 30 percent of the total remuneration of employees in Japan. Growth of total wages per worker grew by just 0.2 percent year-on-year in the last three months of 1992, the lowest rise on record. The earnings crunch reflected flat winter bonuses and a large drop in overtime worked, which was down 17 percent year-on-year. Summer 1993 bonuses were also flat if not actually negative. The trend is actually deteriorating.

Now, it is true that the large share of total remuneration accounted for by bonuses and overtime gives Japanese employers some valuable flexibility in terms of their ability to reduce labor costs, though it will not be enough to stave off outright dismissals in this cycle. But it is also true that actual declines in take-home pay stemming from flat bonuses and steep cuts in overtime exacerbate consumer caution among those in work. This has clearly been the major cause so far of the weakness in consumer spending. Since consumption accounts for 56 percent of the GNP it is hard to see a real economic recovery taking place until it revives. Yet consumers are unlikely to start spending freely again until corporate profits rebound and companies become more generous. But it will require a more pronounced restructuring than anything that has so far been announced for that earnings turnaround to happen. And such a restructuring will at first serve to depress further consumer sentiment because of the unexpected rise in unemployment that will inevitably be a part of it. This is the vicious circle that Japan now finds itself in. It will take some time to get out of. And in the meantime no one should underestimate the psychological shock to the consumer of seeing major companies firing employees for the first time since the Second World War. This is not what is supposed to happen in Japan.

If dwindling remuneration is the main reason for consumer caution there are three other aggravating factors. They are the wealth effect, high levels of consumer debt and the Japanese penchant for fads. Plunging share prices, and more importantly, plunging land prices have clearly contributed to a general sense of caution in recent years. Land prices were still falling in the middle of 1993. Worse, the total lack of transparency in this market, in terms of knowing what the true market-clearing price of a piece of property really is, will have only served to heighten anxiety in a country where only four years ago 99 percent of the population blindly accepted the premise that Japanese land values could never fall even though at that time the total estimated market value of Japanese real estate represented about 60 percent of world property values. That so many people could have accepted such a gross valuation anomaly, and worse borrowed against those collateralized values, can only be viewed as one of financial history's most extreme forms of mass delusion. Individuals, like companies, who borrowed heavily using land pledged as collateral valued at late 1980s prices are clearly now in deep trouble. They are among the worst victims of the Bubble. However, though consumer debt rose sharply in the late

1980s, most Japanese households retain substantial savings, a testament to their traditional frugality. So the net effect is not as disastrous as it might first appear. By March 1991 Japanese gross consumer debt had reached ¥67 trillion or seven times its level at the end of 1979, according to the EPA. This gave Japan a higher gross consumer debt per capita figure than America. Not surprisingly, as a result of this large surge in consumer debt there has since been a sharp rise in personal bankruptcies. However, the average Japanese household at the end of 1990 had ¥8.1 million of savings, a far higher figure than in America. This is a reflection of the Japanese people's penchant for saving, a habit that makes sense given the relative lack of private pension provisions. This traditional frugality was temporarily abandoned during the Bubble years when Japan went on an orgy of consumption. But it has now reasserted itself with a vengeance. The savings rate has started rising again and prudence as a virtue has itself become a fad. The whole process of discount shopping and searching for bargains has become positively trendy in Japan in the early 1990s. Just how trendy is clear from the roaring success of a surprise best-seller that espouses an anti-materialistic almost ascetic theme. Entitled *The Philosophy of Noble Poverty* by Koji Nakano, a Yokohama-based writer, this book sold six hundred thousand copies within six months after being published in September 1992.

There is good reason for this fad beyond pure hype. Japanese households are glutted with consumer durables. Over 99 percent of Japanese households now own refrigerators, televisions and telephones. And over 78 percent own their own car, which is very high given both the crowded circumstances of urban Japan and the cost of parking. The obvious way to get out of this impasse is to deregulate the land market, a process that would enable the Japanese people to live in both bigger and cheaper homes. More money would then be spent on buying bigger houses and doing them up, the fa-

vored preoccupations of the middle classes in developed countries, and less would be frittered away on often useless gadgets
and appliances. For the Japanese shopped until they dropped
during the Bubble years. They now realize that too often they
received little value when handing out their hard-earned
money. It will take a lot to persuade them to start spending it
again. Hence the importance of deregulation.

However, such deregulation of the land and housing market will require a far bolder approach to economic policy
making. Such an approach remains almost totally lacking. For
the bureaucracy has continued to fail to rise to the challenge
posed by Japan's structural crisis. Instead it has clung for too
long to the illusion that the downturn was just another inventory cycle. This harsh judgment is justified given the unimag-
inative nature of the two major fiscal packages announced
despite the startling headline figure of ¥23.9 trillion, which,
according to Finance Ministry propaganda, is the amount that
is supposed to have been pumped into the economy as a
result of these two supplementary budgets. The second budget of ¥13.2 trillion, announced in April 1993 nine months
after the ¥10.7 trillion effort of August 1992, was better than
its predecessor in that it contained more genuine stimulus.
Still, Noboru Kawai, Morgan Stanley's Japanese economist,
reckons the amount of net new spending was still no more
than ¥6 trillion as opposed to only ¥4 trillion in the preceding supplementary effort. Much of the rest of the money is
either conditional and so may not be spent in its entirety, or
accounted for by reclassification of existing spending. The
scope for considerable double counting stems from the com-
plexity of the overlap in Japanese budget accounting between
general and local government as well as spending by the Fiscal Investment and Loan Program (FILP). The FILP, often
referred to as a "second budget," has been aptly described by
Professor Yukio Noguchi of Hitotsubashi University as a
"unique and powerful policy tool" possessed by the Japanese

government.* It is certainly one that other national governments do not possess. It is also a sign of its use that the FILP's
coffers have been tapped of late not only to fund supplementary budgets but also indirectly to support the stock market,
of which more later.

The FILP is essentially a device for rechanneling the
excess savings of the Japanese public for the purpose of operating a government-funded financing plan. Its main element consists of the long-term lending of funds that have
accumulated in the Finance Ministry's trust fund bureau. This
shadowy entity manages ¥292 trillion of public sector funds
including the ¥166 trillion deposited in the giant piggy bank
that is Japan's postal savings system as well as the surpluses
accumulated in the state's insurance and pension plans. In
this sense the Japanese government has ready access to a
huge amount of cash as a result of the public sector running its
own financial services businesses, which compete directly
with banks and insurance companies in the private sector.
However, money used from this source for government-
financing purposes consists of funds already in circulation in
the economy. It therefore does not represent a genuine
stimulus in the form of net new demand.

The Finance Ministry deliberately exaggerates the stimulatory effects of its fiscal packages because it wants to generate the greatest amount of positive psychological effect for
the amount of new money actually spent. If the total sum is
inflated the second supplementary budget, like the first, was
heavily dominated by government public works spending.
Income tax cuts were conspicuously absent. Yet public works
spending can only be of limited impact since even with this
latest increase it still only accounts for 7 percent of the GNP
compared with private capital spending's still far higher share.
Also, building new roads, airports, *shinkansen* bullet-train

* *"The Role of the Fiscal Investment and Loan Program in the Post-War
Japanese Economic Growth," January 1993.*

lines or indeed concrete walls in the middle of paddy fields, which are now visible eyesores in the Japanese countryside, will do little in itself to ease the continuing problems in the banking system or the depressed property market—let alone the overinvestment by corporate Japan. The banks and property owners need rather a long period of low real interest rates for health to be restored.

Yet in the other main component of economic policy making, monetary policy, the Bank of Japan has throughout this period remained stubbornly reactive rather than proactive despite the escalating problems. For its setting of interest rates has continually lagged behind market expectations. The central bank, for example, was seemingly forced into a three quarters of a percentage point cut in the official discount rate (ODR) to 2.5 percent in February 1993. This was the same symbolic level as gave rise to the Bubble Economy in the first place. But this ODR cut was only announced after what had all the trappings of an orchestrated public campaign to discredit the central bank's hardline governor, Yasushi Mieno, an austere career central banker and the man who has deservedly won the reputation for bursting the Bubble. For on assuming the central bank governorship at the end of 1989 Mieno quickly raised interest rates. This policy, coupled with strict quantitative credit controls on property lending, proved extremely effective. The problem was that Mieno subsequently indulged in monetary overkill. He kept the brakes on too long partly because he was so keen to make up for what he viewed rightly as the excessive monetary laxity of the previous central bank governor, the Finance Ministry–appointed Satoshi Sumita, but also partly because he totally failed to comprehend the debt deflationary nature of this cycle and what that meant for money supply growth, the financial system and the economy. Consequently, throughout the period of monetary easing, which began in 1991 and which may still have further to go, ODR cuts have continuously lagged the markets' expectations of what was required. Likewise, the central bank's research department has consistently underestimated the extent of economic weakness primarily because it did not understand the constraints on credit creation posed by debt deflation.

Not surprisingly, the Bank of Japan's hard-line policy has meant that Mieno has made enemies among those who were suffering financially because of the unexpected severity of the downturn. This has led to the inevitable conspiracy theories as to the central bank governor's motives. It is most likely that Mieno simply misread the economy. But there is another view that the central bank has also been pursuing a sociopolitical as well as a monetary agenda. That is to use monetary policy to promote political reform and end Bubble-style speculation and associated dirty-money politics in a country increasingly marred by scandals and policy-making paralysis.

Belief in this second motive might explain the unprecedented public campaign against Mieno in the weeks leading up to the February 1993 ODR cut. First, the Japanese weekly press reported that there was a Finance Ministry "old boy" campaign to get rid of Mieno. It was noted that then prime minister Kiichi Miyazawa, himself supposedly a prime plotter, was a former Finance Ministry official. One press article tenuously linked Mieno's older brother, Tsukasa Mieno, who works for the giant Norinchukin agricultural cooperative where farmers deposit their savings, with the massive debts incurred by Japan's eight housing loan companies to whom the Norinchukin was a major lender and whose debts were then being rescheduled. Another article sought to embarrass the Bank of Japan about the leaking of a confidential document supplied to the central bank by Mitsubishi Bank concerning potential merger candidates for that city bank. *Asahi Shimbun*, a national daily newspaper that first broke the story, sat on the two-year-old document for at least two months before publication while journalists debated whether their pro-Mieno paper should further what was viewed as an orchestrated campaign against the central bank governor. Finally almost everyone who matters in Japan, from politicians to businessmen to bankers, publicly called for an ODR cut. By the time the central bank finally acted the effect of all this was to have cast widespread doubt over whether the Bank of Japan was any longer in control of monetary policy. This means that the central bank may have already lost the considerable degree of independence that Mieno, by virtue of his personal authority alone, had so recently won for it. For legally the Bank of Japan is certainly no Bundesbank, the German central bank which is famous for its independence. Indeed, its powers are legally defined by a 1942 statute based on the Nazi Reichsbank law. The Nazis did not believe in independent central banks. So when the chips are down the far more politically aware Finance Ministry has the power to tell the Bank of Japan what to do.

By the summer of 1993 yet another monetary easing had become inevitable. Once again the central bank seemed to be erring on the side of excessive optimism in terms of its hopes for the economy. Like the EPA it assumed wrongly that the economy had already bottomed and that therefore there would be no need to cut the ODR again. The central bank would therefore not act unless a renewed economic downturn was confirmed by a renewed decline in industrial production. Yet by targeting the real economy and not financial indicators, the Bank of Japan was choosing to ignore the persistence in Japan of high real interest rates (i.e., the cost of money after taking into account the level of inflation). Nominal interest rates may now seem low in Japan, with the ODR back at the all-time low it reached before the Bubble, but in real terms interest rates have continued to rise as a result of growing deflationary pressure reflected in falling wholesale prices. Furthermore, the strength of the yen and retailers' increasingly scanty profit margins were prompting widespread discounting, exacerbating these deflationary forces. Consequently Japan now faces the prospect of falling consumer prices, a development that would be extremely damaging to say the least for corporate profits and therefore for the economy in general despite the gains that would be registered in terms of consumers' real purchasing power.

This is not necessarily to raise the specter of a 1930s-style Great Depression in Japan. It has become increasingly clear that the economic climate of the early 1990s bears more resemblance to the long deflationary period that gripped much of the industrializing world between the mid-1870s and the mid-1890s. This was a twenty-year period of falling prices and rising unemployment, though those lucky enough to be in work enjoyed rising wages. Yet it was not a depression as such since it was not a period of sharply negative GNP growth, though there were periodic rolling depressions in particular markets such as there also have have been in recent years. Take real estate. The property downturn began in Texas and the other American energy states in the early-to-mid-1980s, moved on to financial centers like London and New York in the late 1080s and then rolled on into California, Tokyo and Osaka. The symptoms may have been different in each case but it was the same deflationary trend.

There is certainly no doubt that the prospect, and in many cases the reality, of falling prices in Japan will place substantial further downward pressure on corporate profits. It therefore poses a major challenge not only to policy makers but also to even the most competent of managements. Yet in Japan too many of the senior managers at major companies have long since turned into mere time-serving administrators, the natural result of the bureaucratic inertia bred by lifetime employment and the seniority system. Consequently, they have no idea how to respond to the new challenges save to appeal to the government to pump-prime the economy. This is not how a healthy private sector is supposed to behave in such circumstances.

The strength of the deflationary pressures means that if the Bank of Japan does not move fast enough the Finance Ministry will be forced to step in and order still more ODR cuts. For rising real interest rates are the worst possible medicine in an economy sagging under the burden of debt deflation, which is why America's Federal Reserve has in recent years been targeting real interest rates, among other indicators, in its conduct of monetary policy. For the horror of falling prices lies in the impact it has on the real cost of borrowing and on the real amount of money owed. If prices are falling by, say, 10 percent annually, real interest rates are 10 percent even if the nominal rate of interest is zero. Another cut in the ODR became certain by the late summer of 1993 when the Bank of Japan's expectations of an economy "bumping along the bottom," as the cliché had it, were demolished by a renewed drop in industrial production. A three-quarters-of-a-percentage-point cut in the ODR to 1.75 percent was announced in September 1993 amid clear signs that industrial production, the central bank's favorite indicator, was falling again. But again the ODR cut had been delayed for so long that the stock market, then at a level of 20,000 on the Nikkei and again trading on a scary Bubble-like one hundred times prospective earnings to March 1994, barely rose when the monetary easing was announced. Mieno was still around to announce this further cut, which was a reminder of how wrong he had been on the supposed resilience of the economy. And he may well have to cut yet again, prompted by a further weakening in the economy and/or a renewed plunge in a stock market that is dangerously divorced in terms of its valuation from economic reality. The central bank governor will most likely from now on tamely do

the Finance Ministry's bidding partly because his credibility
has been shot and partly because his term as governor expires
in December 1994. Ultimately, Mieno is a part of the system
he grew up in. A true maverick does not become governor of
as conservative an institution as the Bank of Japan.

Monetary policy is only one aspect of economic policy
making, though a vitally important one. On the fiscal front, as
noted earlier, a third supplementary budget of ¥6.1 trillion
was announced in September 1993 of even more limited scope
than the previous two packages. This again will not do the
trick. It will take the scare and specter of rising unemployment to goad the bureaucracy into real action. Then the final
stimulus when it comes is likely to be genuinely enormous,
which means that the Finance Ministry's usual laudable concerns about deficit financing will be thrown to the wind. There
will be long-overdue income tax cuts to stimulate consumer
spending combined with some kind of Japanese version of
America's New Deal of the 1930s, though with a 1990s technological slant. A hint of what this may look like can be found
in a ten-year ¥100 trillion infrastructure plan that has already
been floated by MITI and that has been described as Japan's
Tennessee Valley Authority (TVA), probably the most famous
of the New Deal projects. The MITI proposal is not just for
the usual physical infrastructure. Rather, the main thrust is a
plan to build a so-called electronic highway linking every Japanese household by optic fiber cable. This sort of plan will at
some point be taken up enthusiastically, for by then it will
have become clear to the bureaucracy that its own survival is
at stake. It will also be justified by the argument that Japan is
slipping behind, as it is, in the fast-developing "hot" area of
multimedia information technology as a result of silly domestic regulations that are caused by bureaucratic turf battles
rather than industrial logic.

Japan remains to a remarkable extent considering its economic clout a passive spectator in the growing trend to merge voice communications with moving images and other data, which is after all what multimedia is meant to be all about. However, the government's likely attempt to go high-tech via some form of national plan will have the usual bureaucratic defect. It will mark an effort to pump-prime the economy out of its slump by spending taxpayers' money in the conviction that officialdom knows best. Whereas the best way forward would be to deregulate and let private business make the decisions. Information technology, which will be the backbone of the early twenty-first-century economy, is not an area suited to *dirigiste* economic policy making, be it on the French, Soviet or Japanese models.

But by the time this huge fiscal boost is announced, Japan's bureaucracy, at the apex of which is the Finance Ministry, will be pulling out all the stops. For it will by then have received the shock of its life in the sense of finally waking up to the structural problems facing the country. And it will be fighting to preserve its own privileged power base in a status quo under mounting attack. For the continued failure of officials to understand the depth and nature of the economic problems and so deal with them effectively, combined with their instincts to re-regulate at the first hint of trouble, will have caused a profound loss of confidence among both companies and consumers in the bureaucracy's competence, especially the Finance Ministry's. Indeed the ministry will increasingly be compared with that military white elephant, the ill-fated battleship *Yamato* (the 72,000-ton monster which was sunk south of Okinawa in 1945) in terms of the increasingly disastrous direction it has led the rest of Japan, a historical comparison that is entirely appropriate.

This raises the key question of whether Japanese officialdom's exalted status will survive the end of Japan Inc. The answer is that the bureaucrats will survive since civil servants are necessary evils in modern society. But their status will not. In the meantime, nowhere has this urge to re-regulate and prevent the emergence of clear winners and losers been more apparent than in a financial system that remains by American standards primitive. The result will be that Japan, a country with the highest savings rate in the industrialized world, will continue to suffer from gross inefficiencies in the allocation of capital.

4

Financial System—
Still Deflating

THERE IS JUST a chance that Japan's financial crisis
reached its nadir in August 1992 when the Nikkei stock market
index plunged to near the 14,000 level, some 60 percent below
its all-time high. At this shrunken level the integrity of the financial system itself was in question, since many major banks
and also many major life insurance companies had by then no
capital gains left on their long-term shareholdings. This mattered for the banks because the capital gains they hold on their
long-term shareholdings are about their only effective buffer
against bad debts, given their still minimal level of loan-loss
reserves. Japan's big banks, which just a few years ago seemed
poised to take over the world, were suddenly left wondering
where all their money had gone.

The disappearance of capital gains was equally as life-
threatening for the life insurers, Japan's other financial behe-
moths. For their solvency was also suddenly in question.
Since 1945 life insurance companies have paid policyholders
out of cash flow. Money flowing into the general account has
always exceeded the money paid out. Much slower growth in
assets and net new business, combined with too generous
guaranteed payouts made during a period of higher interest
rates, now threatened this cozy arrangement. Hence the

growing fears prompted by the stock market's slump that life insurers would be forced into massive selling of securities to meet policyholders' claims. Yet as their capital gains vanished so did their buttress against just such an emergency.

The government averted this late-summer crisis with the twin announcements, brought forward hastily, of the first supplementary budget, worth some ¥10.7 trillion, and of an official support plan to inject public sector funds into the stock market. In late September a total of ¥1.7 trillion of beneficiaries' money held in public sector savings institutions was handed over to institutional investors, principally trust banks, to invest in shares. The funds came from the postal insurance fund, the postal savings fund and the national pension system, which is also run through the post office. A further ¥1.1 trillion was released in November. The trust banks, emboldened by considerable political prodding, were given every incentive to invest in shares. Rather than meet an annual performance target as is usual, they were given five years in which to earn an average annual return of 5.5 percent. This means their investment performance will not be measured until September 1997 by when, it is hoped, the bear market will be a distant (though no doubt still painful) memory.

Stockbrokers were quick to give the government's politically inspired stock market support effort a catchy name. They called it the PKO (price-keeping operation), a term borrowed from Japan's peacekeeping operation in Cambodia conducted under the United Nations umbrella. The exercise's apparent success at putting a floor under the stock market soon encouraged officials to allocate more funds to the effort. For the fiscal year that began in March 1993 a further ¥6.6 trillion was allocated to the support operation. However, precisely how much public sector money was being spent propping up share prices was fast becoming beside the point. For increasingly investors were prepared to assume the government had underwritten the market until such time as a genuine earnings rebound occurred as a result of a recovering economy, which would justify the stock market's still extremely lofty level of valuation.

The stock market support operation was also accompanied by a veritable blizzard of administrative guidance, since the bureaucrats in the ever-meddling Finance Ministry were prepared to leave nothing to chance in their efforts to prevent further financial distress. There was a frenzy of improvization to plug all possible holes prior to the conclusion of the financial year that ended in March 1993. This is the key date in the corporate calendar because it is when balance sheets are drawn up and capital ratios fixed. Thus, the life insurance companies were told by the Finance Ministry in January 1993 that they could use unrealized capital gains to pay dividends to policyholders that year. This amounted to a temporary revision of Japan's insurance law, which states that life insurers can only pay policyholders out of income, not capital gains. Clearly, paying dividends out of only paper capital gains that could disappear should share prices subsequently fall seems extraordinarily imprudent.

But perhaps the most effective intervention of all was the blatant politically inspired ramping of the share price of NTT, Japan's domestic telephone utility and the company with the highest stock market valuation in the world. This did more than any other measures taken to buy precious time for the Tokyo stock market, and hence for the Japanese financial system, while the economy remained so depressed. Assume that Wall Street was mired in a three-year bear market and the share price of IBM, once corporate America's flagship stock, suddenly doubled in price in three months. This is precisely what happened in Japan in the spring of 1993. NTT is in fact much more important to the Tokyo market than a shrunken IBM now is to Wall Street. It was the stock that symbolized Japan's roaring bull market of the second half of the 1980s. The company was first floated by a greedy Japanese government in 1986 in a sales pitch aimed at small investors. The offer price was ¥1.2 million per share, which put NTT then on a prospective price-earnings ratio of 133. Two more tranches of shares were subsequently sold in 1987 and 1988. Retail investors were eager purchasers of the Tokyo market's biggest share. NTT's share price peaked at ¥3.2 million in April 1987 when the telephone company was valued at ¥12.2 trillion—more than the Italian stock market's then total capitalization. But the experience did not prove a happy one for most investors who bought shares in the three public offerings at an average share price of ¥1.9 million. NTT's stock subsequently declined by more than 80 percent to reach a low of ¥453,000 in August 1992.

So precipitous a decline, combined with the fact that a relatively high level of shares was owned by small investors who had bought them from the government, made NTT's share price a sensitive political issue. This explains politicians' real concerns about the matter. Kabun Muto, chairman of the LDP's tax affairs council, publicly gave notice of what was to come in early 1993 when he said that the government had a duty to raise the telephone company's share price at least to its initial first offering price of ¥1.2 million. This was not just wishful thinking. Unlike most private companies the profitability of NTT is almost entirely at the government's discretion, since it sets the rates that NTT charges for local calls. So what better way to boost its share price, and indeed the whole stock market, than by allowing NTT to raise its charges. This is exactly what Muto went on to recommend. He was soon joined in this campaign by NTT's president, Masahski Kojima. These proposals were soon followed by managed press leaks indicating that such a domestic rate hike was indeed under consideration. By this time most well-informed politicians had already loaded up on NTT's shares.

Such a rate hike was indeed justified since NTT's local call rates had not been increased since 1987. It was also true that the resulting boost to its profits would be considerable. Still, the whole exercise looked extremely political. Yet even with the benefit of this ramp and the subsequent announcement of the rate hike, NTT's share price only managed to reach a high at the peak of its 1993 rally that was barely above its initial offering price before sliding back again. Presumably many insiders sold once the news was out and the ¥1.2 million target had been just about reached. Still, the explosion in the NTT share price succeeded in pushing the market up to just over the 21,000 level in May 1993. This may have been a long way below the Nikkei's all-time high of nearly 40,000 but it represented in percentage terms a significant rebound from the lows reached the previous August.

By this time the vast majority of investment pundits had long concluded, prematurely, that the bear market was over and that it was from now on just a matter of how quickly the stock market would advance. Yet a closer look at who had been buying and selling Japanese shares during the spring rally made the stock market's advance look as suspect as the blatant government rigging would suggest it was. Thus, during the six weeks from the beginning of March when the Nikkei share average made most of its gains, foreign investors and Japanese individuals buying on credit or "margin" accounted for virtually all the net buying. Foreign investors bought a net ¥613 billion worth of shares between February 25 and April 7 on the Tokyo, Osaka and Nagoya stock exchanges, and margin investors bought a net ¥568 billion with many of them piling into NTT. By contrast, Japanese financial institutions and other sorts of Japanese companies were net sellers, as were small investors dealing in cash.

The difference can be explained by foreign investors' still excessive confidence in the Japanese government's ability to work miracles by supporting the stock market and their still premature hopes of an imminent economic rebound in the second half of that year. By contrast, Japan's professional investors remained innately cautious and clearly used the rally as an opportunity to unload shares at prices many of them would not have dared hope for six months earlier. These institutional investors, such as the life insurance companies, had good reason to remain cautious. It was after all only a few months previously that their unrealized capital gains had almost been wiped out. If they purchased shares at higher levels and the market subsequently fell back again, then the average purchase cost of their portfolio would have been raised that much higher, increasing the risk of disaster the next time the stock market collapsed. In this context to miss out on a rally seemed less disastrous than to risk financial ruin. This is why the bearish consensus among Japan's institutional investors will not be so easily broken, especially as they are more intimately familiar with the gory details of what is really going on inside many Japanese companies than are the foreigners. After straying all over the investment world buying lots of exotic securities during the 1980s, the life insurers in particular had no stomach for risk. Their aim was to put as many of their assets as possible in hopefully safe yen loans and bonds, however low the yield earned.

Yet the Finance Ministry did not concern itself with such considerations. Instead its interventions were becoming increasingly shameless. Not content with rigging the stock market, the bureaucrats could not resist pushing to impose unprecedented and arbitrary controls on stock index futures trading. The mandarins have continued to view the futures market as a playground for naughty stockbrokers, especially foreign ones, rather than a place where risk is managed. At the Finance Ministry's bidding the Tokyo Stock Exchange (TSE) in March 1993 proposed sweeping changes. The securities firms first heard about the proposals at a TSE committee on derivatives. Some of them seemed quite reasonable, including more disclosure of trading activities and the introduction of American-style circuit breakers where a market is shut automatically for a period after it declines by a certain percentage during a trading day. It was the rest that floored the listening brokers. The TSE wanted to be able to ban arbitrage and proprietary trading (which accounts for about 65 percent of total trading volume) in stock index futures whenever it thinks the futures market is "overheated or has the risk of getting overheated." The exchange went on to define "overheated" in the broadest and most arbitrary of terms, such as whenever the prices of stock index futures fluctuate "significantly" or when speculative transactions exceed a certain proportion of all trades. The TSE officials even told the astonished assembled brokers that the market had been "overheated" from September 1990 to December 1991. Stockbrokers could only conclude that the proposals as stated meant that the TSE wanted to be able to halt most futures trading whenever share prices looked like they could fall sharply.

This threat to stop firms, almost on a whim, from buying and selling stock index futures caused some alarm. If securities firms face the risk that they will themselves be unable to close positions they will naturally be far less willing to commit their own capital to trading in the futures market. This was presumably the exchange's intention. But it is likely to hurt more than the handful of foreign brokers that officials love to hate. American securities firms such as Morgan Stanley and Salomon Brothers have indeed profited most in recent years from trading futures in Japan by exploiting their superior technology developed on Wall Street. Many foreign brokers have relied on futures to support their losses on ordinary agency stockbroking during Tokyo's long bear market. But big Japanese brokers such as Nomura and Daiwa would also be hurt, which is why they also disliked the TSE's heavyhanded proposals. For they have become more active in stock index futures in a bid to emulate the success of their gaijin competitors. A cynic would even say that they have been able profitably to trade futures ahead of big buy orders made by the

Japanese fund managers charged with investing public sector pension funds allocated to the stock market.

Yet despite such widespread opposition to the plan, the TSE seemed serious. Certainly, foreign firms who complained to the Finance Ministry were told disingenuously to take their case to the TSE. If the proposals are implemented (and enough firms do not find Singapore's Simex futures exchange, where the Nikkei contract is also traded, an acceptable alternative), it will help suck liquidity out of the futures market and therefore make the Tokyo stock market a more dangerous place the next time investors panic as they assuredly will— exactly the reverse of what Japanese officialdom seems to believe. For in recent years the futures market has absorbed a lot of selling pressure arising in the stock market. Institutional investors who are able to hedge their equity holdings (by selling futures) are less likely to sell their shares outright. The TSE and its Finance Ministry sponsors are also wrong to be so suspicious of the predominance of proprietary trading in stock index futures. It is mainly explained by the absence of "locals"—the term used in Chicago, the world capital of futures trading, to describe individual floor traders making prices in a trading pit—from the Osaka Stock Exchange on whose computerized trading system the Nikkei stock index futures contract is bought and sold in Japan. For locals and proprietary traders serve the same healthy purpose. That is to provide liquidity. Thus, on the Chicago Mercantile Exchange, locals account for around half of total trading volume in the S&P 500 stock index futures contract, and member securities firms dealing for their own account for another 15 percent. Their combined share is about the same as that of securities firms' proprietary trading in the Osaka Nikkei contract.

But such esoteric arguments are lost on the backwoodsmen at the TSE. They think that foreign securities firms have scared away small investors from the stock market by their shenanigans and have made obscene profits in doing so. They have been encouraged in this belief by the smaller Japanese securities firms who do not understand the new futures technology and who have themselves been losing lots of money. The worrying point of course is that big institutional investors, be they foreign or domestic, risk losing their ability to hedge their positions in what is still the world's second biggest stock market at precisely the moment they will probably most want to sell. That is when the Nikkei is falling sharply. And it will fall sharply again when the stock market realizes belatedly that economic recovery is still a long way off.

The direct rigging of the stock market, the increasingly prevalent attempt to use administrative guidance techniques such as arbitrary changes in accounting rules to prevent shares being sold at a loss or underwater investments being marked-to-market, and the increasingly absurd attack on the futures markets all form part of a trend. That is an increasingly overt attempt by the Finance Ministry to re-regulate.

By the middle of 1993 the mandarins at the Finance Ministry had begun to gloat. After presiding since 1990 over a series of humiliating banking and securities scandals, not to mention shaming policy failures, they had begun to feel vindicated again. They were lauded for pumping up the economy with the second supplementary budget and for "rescuing" the Japanese stock market by ordering public sector savings institutions to buy Japanese shares. This was all grist to the mill to those foreign observers of Japan who like to argue that Japan has been so successful because it works by different rules than does the West. Administrative guidance was back with a vengeance, they asserted approvingly. And officialdom showed disturbing signs of believing the flatterers. It will have proved a Pyrric victory, for the celebrations were way too premature, both for the stock market and the economy. They came as the latest leap in the yen only added to the deflationary pressures already bearing down upon Japan's economy.

The Finance Ministry had in fact made a major mistake. For it assumed, wrongly, that the most effective way out of Japan's troubles was to indulge in what is anyway its strongest instinct. That is to re-regulate everything, a process that also has the benefit of consolidating the ministry's own power. It has become increasingly obvious that this is precisely the direction in which the ministry is heading again. The Finance Ministry seems intent on retaining a degree of centralized bureaucratic control wholly inconsistent with what is normally implied by the term deregulation. As a result, Japan risks being saddled with the same primitive financial services industry that created the late 1980s boom-bust cycle. That is an industry with a nannylike dependence on bureaucratic guidance and where clear winners and losers are not allowed to emerge, as they have, say, in Japan's auto and electronics industries. That will lead to a continuing lack of product innovation and a further loss of competitiveness. Japanese banks and securities firms remain far behind their American and even European counterparts. Capital will continue to be allocated inefficiently in Japan; and risk will be measured badly if not at all. Regulatory overkill explains why Japan still has no efficient corporate bond market though it desperately needs one since the banks want now only to lend to the safest credits, while the stock market has remained virtually closed to new equity issues since early 1990 because of officialdom's concern that added supply would further depress share prices. Stifling regulation and traditional hidebound attitudes also explain why Japan has not properly exploited securitization, an available technology, which as America's example in recent years has shown has the potential to alleviate at least some of the distress in Japan's property market.

The increasingly pro-regulatory bias is also clear concerning the development of the financial services industry. After years of tortuous study of the issue, the resulting move to break down barriers between banks and brokers has been almost pathetic in its limited scope. Stockbroking commissions also remain fixed. And the pace of deregulation in the cartelized insurance industry is glacial. The way the Finance Ministry proposes to manage Japan's bad-debt problem also shows it is committed to maintaining its traditional convoy approach toward the banking industry. Thus, to encourage those banks that can afford it aggressively to reserve against questionable loans or write dud ones off would unmask glaring qualitative differences between institutions, which officials would be most unhappy about. The unmasking of losses would also naturally have another effect. It would cause the public to focus more on the bad-debt mess and, as a consequence, on the Finance Ministry's own responsibility for letting it happen.

Just as the drive to re-regulate was encouraged by the view that renewed intervention seemed to be working, so did it promote a belief that it was back to business as normal. Take Nomura, Japan's biggest securities firm. It was clear to insiders by the middle of 1993 that the firm was effectively being run day to day by Yoshihisa ("Little") Tabuchi. Tabuchi is the disgraced former president who resigned in the heat of the 1991 scandals involving loss-compensation payments and dealings with organized crime. Yet he has retained ever since an office at the firm in his official capacity as a "senior adviser" and, by all accounts, has continued to tell the current president, Hideo Sakamaki, what to do. A samurai-like figure of the old school, Tabuchi may no longer be so popular among Nomura's employees at large, especially its younger turks. But Sakamaki and most of the current board of directors owe their lofty positions to him and have evidently remained loyal. Tabuchi still even harbors ambitions to become chairman when the present figurehead chairman, Yukio Aida, retires in 1994. The schoolmasterly Aida was brought out of retirement to take on the top job in 1991 when former chairman Setsuya "Big" Tabuchi (no relation) also resigned as a result of the securities scandals. That Little Tabuchi even thought such a formal return to prominence was possible shows the extent to which he at least had begun to assume matters were back to normal. The grip of the Big Four securities firms certainly remained as strong as ever. Nomura, Daiwa, Nikko and Yamaichi had an 83 percent share of domestic underwriting fees in the financial year that ended in March 1993. They also had a 30 percent share of agency broking commissions.

Still, profits rather than market share are now the issue since red ink has been gushing from the Japanese securities industry as a result of the three-year-long bear market and plummeting stock market trading volume. Only Nomura managed to make money (just) at the net profit level in the financial year that ended in March 1993, a period when the average daily turnover on the Tokyo Stock Exchange was only 286 million shares. Most securities firms need daily volume of at least 500 million shares to stay out of the red. There is a limit to how long this financial hemorrhaging can go on without major layoffs or waves of forced mergers. The big brokers have already slashed investment spending on items like computerized trading systems. And they have been able to reduce their personnel costs somewhat by cutting bonuses and overtime work without actually firing employees. Graduate recruitment is also way down. Nomura cut its graduate intake from 1,002 to 606 in 1993. Some of the smaller brokers, less encumbered by notions of lifetime employment, have shed employees quite aggressively by Japanese standards. Yet there still remained 142,000 people employed in the securities industry at the end of March 1993, according to the Japan Securities Dealers Association, down by less than 20,000 from the 162,000 people employed at the peak in March 1990. This is not much of a pruning given that many broking firms outside the Big Four will soon go out of business if they continue to lose money at the current rate. This suggests forced mergers ahead with strong brokers or even banks taking over the weak, as Daiwa Bank took over loss-ridden Cosmo Securities in August 1993, though presumably only after the Finance Ministry has given its required approval. By way of contingency planning for such an outcome, from April 1, 1993, Japanese banks were allowed to own 100 percent of a securities firm, as opposed to only 5 percent previously.

Meanwhile, as with the banks, there doubtless remain many unexploded bombs still lurking off-balance-sheet in the securities companies, given the protracted viciousness of the bear market. For example, detailed rumors of serious financial problems have continued to circulate about Yamaichi Securities, Japan's fourth largest securities company, which employs 11,600 people. The persistent rumors may possibly be an unfair legacy of history: Yamaichi was Japan's biggest stockbroker until it was rescued from bankruptcy in 1965 by a bailout led by the Bank of Japan. Organized by the central bank, three banks—Industrial Bank of Japan, Fuji Bank and Mitsubishi Bank—lent money to Yamaichi. But there does seem to be something newly amiss at Yamaichi if only because it is suffering greater losses than its Big Four peers. The rumor has it that Yamaichi's losses have been compounded by so-called *tobashi* commitments. *Tobashi* is a form of share-repurchase agreement used by Japanese brokers to shift unhealthy-looking investments from one client to another— Cosmo also had *tobashi* problems. Needless to say, Yamaichi has denied categorically that it has any *tobashi* arrangements, especially that it has outstanding *tobashi* commitments to buy back hundreds of billions of yen worth of shares from two major Japanese companies, a carmaker and a construction company. This is not immaterial since Yamaichi only had net cash holdings—cash deposits minus short-term borrowings—of ¥94 billion at the end of September 1992.

If Yamaichi had never entered into *tobashi* arrangements, that would in itself be surprising. In the late 1980s most Japanese securities firms did engage in such repurchase agreements. The initial trigger was losses incurred in their *eigyo tokkin* accounts following the 1987 stock market crash. *Eigyo tokkin* were a special form of discretionary trading account where the securities firms themselves, rather than investment advisers, managed the money. The securities companies encouraged their corporate clients to set up these *eigyo tokkin* by offering them, at least verbally, guaranteed rates of return. This proved a matter of some controversy. At the end of 1989 the Finance Ministry issued two directives two days before the Nikkei index reached its all-time high. The first ordered the securities firms to end *eigyo tokkin* immediately. The second ordered them to stop compensating investors. This presented a practical problem for the brokers since they could only wind up the *eigyo tokkin* in a manner agreeable to their clients by compensating them for their losses, a problem that grew in size as the Tokyo market proceeded to plunge. By then Yamaichi had already dug itself into a major hole. It had been unwise enough during 1989 to go on increasing the size of its *eigyo tokkin* accounts even though Nomura, for example, began retreating from this business at the end of 1988, wary of continuing to offer guaranteed returns as share prices soared to ever more lunatic levels.

Still, it was the October 1987 crash that caused the first problem for the brokers in terms of honoring the verbal guarantees made on *eigyo tokkin* accounts. Creative minds within the securities firms came up with a solution in the form of *tobashi*. The idea of this form of equity repurchase agreement is to take advantage of companies' different reporting dates. The purpose is to shift underwater securities holdings into other hands when year-end balance sheets are drawn up. The guarantor of the arrangement is the securities firm, which after all is only arranging a *tobashi* because it needs to honor a previous guarantee. A typical *tobashi* arrangement would work as follows. Company A, facing a loss on its investment, moves it to Company B with a different financial year-end reporting date on the understanding that Company A will buy it back paying Company B an agreed amount of "interest" for the service rendered. The problem with such an arrangement is that repurchase agreements based on shares are illegal in Japan. This is why a Yamaichi overseas subsidiary is said to have done the *tobashi* deals with offshore subsidiaries of the companies which acted as counterparties. Such a practice would mean that there is no need to mention such arrangements in a securities firm's accounts. In Yamaichi's case, in fact, the firm's Netherlands subsidiary was apparently the key player in the *tobashi* operation.

Tobashi becomes a problem when no one is willing to buy the share, however attractive the reward offered. That has long since happened. *Tobashi* became public knowledge in 1992 when Daiwa, Japan's second biggest securities firm, announced it would pay ¥73.5 billion to settle lawsuits brought by five companies, all of which concerned *tobashi* arrangements. Since Yamaichi denies categorically any *tobashi* arrangements, this may explain why it has not faced a similar wave of lawsuits. But another explanation could be that Yamaichi has continued to honor its guarantees by making payments out of its own resources. The counterparties in its *tobashi* arrangements also are publicly quoted companies who do not want to see this practice exposed in the law courts. (Note that both the Daiwa and Cosmo cases became public knowledge as a result of litigation.) If Yamaichi is still paying out, it explains why it is losing so much more money than the other three of the Big Four (¥52 billion in the last fiscal year) even though their basic businesses are all broadly the same. Yamaichi has blamed its worse results on unidentified "trading losses." In addition, Yamaichi had only ¥36 billion worth of net unrealized gains on its share portfolio in September 1992 (down from ¥113 billion the previous year) compared with Nomura's ¥296 billion.

Certainly near confirmation that Yamaichi's denials were

indeed suspect came in August 1993 when it emerged that Yamaichi Securities had shifted the yen equivalent of several hundred million dollars from Yamaichi Real Estate into Yamaichi Finance, the subsidiary into which the *tobashi* losses had already been shifted by the parent securities company. Yamaichi's losses are probably about 50 percent of outstanding *tobashi* positions of ¥500–600 billion. Interestingly Masayuki Takagi, a former senior managing director and head of Yamaichi Securities' corporate division, was shifted to Yamaichi Finance to take care of the mess. This was appropriate since Takagi had been the powerful promoter of tokkin funds during the Bubble period. He is also a prototype Japanese securities industry person. He was transferred to the Netherlands subsidiary for five years after the equity offering of Nihon Netsugaku, an air-conditioning equipment maker, went bust less than one year after it was floated on the stock market in 1974. Takagi in this manner earned the gratitude of his bosses since the Finance Ministry at the time was demanding a scapegoat. As a result of his loyalty he was quickly promoted to a key position, namely the head of the corporate division, when he finally returned to Tokyo after a stint in Osaka.

Another pertinent fact that has fueled the rumors which have continued to swirl around the firm is that Yamaichi has no single clear main bank.* Officially Industrial Bank of Japan, Mitsubishi Bank and Fuji Bank are all three main banks. Each owns a 3.6 percent stake in the securities firm. Yet a Yamaichi insider describes the three banks as each being of "equal distance" from the securities company. This hardly suggests a desire to provide unqualified support. During the late 1980s Yamaichi, riding high and arrogant, did a foolish

* *The main bank is the bank which is usually the major lender to the company in question and also the bank which is meant under Japanese convention to stand behind it should this company get into financial difficulty.*

thing for any broker dependent on credit. It distanced itself from its main commercial banks. Thus, three senior ex-IBJ directors, who had been with Yamaichi since the 1965 rescue, were not replaced with IBJ bankers when they retired. Yamaichi also grew apart from Mitsubishi Bank, which anyway is the main bank to Nikko, Japan's third largest securities firm. That probably leaves a reluctant Fuji Bank as the remaining main bank in the event of a problem since Fuji and Yamaichi belong to the same Fuyo keiretsu group of companies. Family ties are not always a blessing.

Meanwhile, whatever unexploded bombs are still concealed in the securities industry, confidence in the government's ability to support the stock market continued to grow, especially among naive foreign investors. The support operation itself also became more aggressive in terms of the tactics employed. One tactic used by the managers of public sector funds was deliberately to pitch buy orders to purchase shares at above the last dealt price. This could be considered rank market manipulation. Yet nobody, save for a few free market purists, seemed to worry, least of all the recently formed Securities and Exchange Surveillance Commission, whose office is located conveniently next to the Finance Ministry. Another tactic was so-called package transactions, where trust banks each buy, say, one hundred thousand shares of the same twenty stocks—all of them key components of the Nikkei index. Another ploy was for the managers of the public money to buy stock index futures at the beginning of a day's trading, which tends to raise the price of the underlying shares and get the day off to a good bullish start. This is known by broker wags as PLOs (price-lifting operations), a variation of PKOs.

The use of such brazen tactics would seem a clear inducement to revive the share-rigging practices, the disclosure of which so embarrassed the Finance Ministry when the securities scandals became public in the summer of 1991. But few within the ranks of officialdom will fret about this. Government policy was quite simply to get the stock market up and, above all, to do whatever it took to prevent it from falling again. For the stock market is no longer disdained by economic policy makers as a vulgar casino not worthy of their attention, the traditional mandarin attitude of both the Finance Ministry and the central bank. Evidence of the official change in attitude came with the publication in February 1993 of a Bank of Japan special paper titled "Functions of Stock Markets: Implications for Corporate Financial Activities." Policy makers now recognized belatedly, albeit correctly, that a rising stock market is one important way of reviving the economy. This makes particular sense in Japan because as the market rises so does the value of the banks' capital, which consists partly of the unrealized gains on their shareholdings.

So a rising stock market literally increases banks' ability to lend. It also increases the net worth of the corporate sector because of the still widespread system of cross shareholding where companies own shares in one another not for the purposes of investment but to cement long-standing business relationships. Higher share prices would also enable companies, which are now suffering from a cash flow squeeze, to raise funds either by selling other companies' shares they own as part of their existing cross shareholdings or by issuing more of their own shares in the same way that a rising American stock market in the early 1990s has allowed so many American companies to reduce their debt levels via the issuance of equity. For the past three years of course the Tokyo stock market has not been fulfilling its prime function as a capital-raising vehicle because of the continued informal Finance Ministry ban on new issues.

The Japanese government's bet seems to be that by rigging the stock market it can improve sentiment sufficiently to lure in enough suckers to pull off the same sort of giant debt for equity swap as has occurred in America. They will probably have to be individual and gaijin investors if this ploy is to pay off. For it is not only banks and life insurers that will remain cautious. Japanese companies will also remain net sellers of shares. The deterioration in these companies' cash flow positions may surprise. But this is now one of the key problems facing both the Japanese stock market and the economy, along with more familiar ailments such as the bad debts in the banking system and the continued distress in the property market. Japanese companies' financing needs are now greater than at any time since the 1974 oil shock. Smithers & Co. has estimated that the cash deficit of the corporate sector will have amounted to about 8 percent of the GNP or ¥40 trillion in 1993, compared with only 2.8 percent in 1988.* Companies so far have been meeting this need partly by drawing down on their cash reserves. Japanese companies' cash holdings declined, for example, at a rate of 7 percent per annum in the last three months of 1992. Meanwhile another way of raising cash, namely by borrowing from the bank, has become much less attractive. For banks in recent years have begun to charge corporate borrowers properly for their loans, as opposed to subsidizing them as they so often did in the past. They have had to in order to boost their operating profits to enable them more easily to cope with their huge bad-debt problems. Consequently, banks' lending rates have not fallen in line with their funding costs as interest rates have fallen. As a result, their lending margins have improved by about two percentage points since early 1991. All of which means a higher cost of borrowing for companies. To finance a cash deficit of ¥40 trillion at a borrowing rate prevailing in mid-1993 of around 5 percent would cost ¥2 trillion per annum. This is a high real cost of borrowing at a time when consumer inflation in Japan is heading below 1 percent.

So with their cash reserves dwindling and the cost of bank

* *"The Japanese Market: Government Support versus Corporate Liquidity."*

credit expanding, companies are likely to accelerate their already steady selling of shares, especially as those shares still yield under 1 percent in terms of the dividends paid at a level of 20,000 on the Nikkei index. This is a rate of return on capital that is hard to defend, especially when companies are increasingly targeting profitability rather than market share. They have to do this because Japanese companies no longer enjoy a cost of capital advantage over their international competitors as a result of the phased deregulation of Japanese interest rates during the 1980s. By 1992 the average cost of capital for Japan had converged to about the same level as for American companies. The significance of this trend is profound, as was recognized by Masasuke Ide, an executive fellow at the Nomura Research Institute, in a study paper.* Ide argued that in the long run the pressure on banks and other financial institutions to earn a better rate of return on their capital will break down the traditional Japanese relationship-based system to one based more on arm's-length negotiations among companies and between companies and financial institutions. "If financial institutions start seeking higher returns for depositors and investors, that will make it very difficult for them to keep supporting the low-return strategy of their traditional corporate partners. That means the entire traditional relationships will have to be reviewed in the new light of financial returns, including the thorough reassessment of the relationship of stock investments and cross-holding arrangements." Or in other words, relationships will no longer matter.

The logical consequence of this change is an end to banks' lending at preferential terms to favored corporate customers, or for that matter banks investing in these companies' shares for relationship reasons. That in turn means it will be hard for Japanese companies to continue to maintain the traditional practices that so many pundits have concluded are the cause

* *The Japanese Financial System and the Competitiveness of Large Japanese Companies.*

of their long-term success; examples are the stress on long-term planning, research and development and heavy capital investment, lifetime employment, and the emphasis on quality and low prices. Much of this was only made possible by Japanese firms' far lower cost of capital as compared with the competition. Now, if the cost of capital has indeed converged, that must also mean Japanese companies will have to behave more like American or European concerns since they will have to be far more focused on profitability. In the long run that should help cause trade disputes to fade, since dumping excess production in export markets should become a far less attractive strategy. In the short term, though, it has dramatic implications for the employment system. For such radical change is always traumatic.

It also has drastic implications for the stock market, for the above circumstances point to an unwinding of Japan's cross-shareholding system. How gradual or not this unwinding will prove will depend on how quickly Japanese corporate profits recover. The longer and steeper the slump the more dramatic will be the dumping of shares. Indeed this process has already begun. Thus, Nissan in September 1993 announced publicly it would be selling outright long-term holdings of shares. Initially, as is only to be expected, companies will sell the shares of those companies with whom they have the most distant business relationships. Shares of close *keiretsu* partners will clearly be the last to be sold.

Among those doing the selling will be the banks, since they, along with the life insurance companies, own about two thirds of the Tokyo stock market and therefore are the major bulwarks of the cross-shareholding system. Japan's banks will be selling because they will remain under financial pressure for years to come, primarily as a consequence of the way their bad-debt problems are being addressed or rather not addressed. The scale of these problems remains immense.

Problem debts in Japan total some ¥60 trillion, though

not all of these rest with the banks. The agricultural credit cooperatives, to give just one example, have lots of questionable debts, the extent of which the world may never know about because of the extreme political sensitivities involved. Even now, long after the problem was first officially recognized, no one really knows the exact size of the bad-debt problem (not even officials at the Finance Ministry or the central bank) because there is no proper system for monitoring them and many individual bank branch managers may not be owning up to them. Consequently, if a bank does not admit to a problem, then the bureaucracy may well not know about it. The problem is more serious than in the West because Japanese banks have by international standards minute loan-loss reserves to set aside against bad debts compared with their international competitors beyond a mandatory reserve of 0.3 percent of total loans. There are two historic reasons for this. First, there has been almost no tax incentive for Japanese banks to reserve against their problem loans since the tax authorities traditionally have only allowed a bank to make such a reserve and deduct it against its taxable income where the borrower is declared officially insolvent. The banks, it should be noted, have long been Japan's biggest taxpayers. Second, loan-loss reserves were considered unnecessary because banks regarded the capital gains on their long-term shareholdings, their so-called hidden reserves, as their effective loan-loss reserves. Needless to say, as these gains have shrunk in size with the stock market's decline so has the banks' ability to withstand the impact of bad debts been reduced.

So the debt problem presents a formidable challenge to a system that no longer really works. Yet the issue of how to own up to these bad credits, let alone pay for them, has yet to be fully addressed. This reflects political as well as financial pressures. Unlike in America, Japan does not have an organized hierarchy of independent bank examiners. Nor is it yet acceptable public policy openly to spend taxpayers' money bailing out banks as American taxpayers, however reluctantly, accepted the need to pay for the savings and loan disaster to prevent an outright depression. And if American depositors in these thrift institutions and similarly insolvent banks had had their savings wiped out there would have been such a depression. The result in Japan has been a continuing official reluctance to own up to the size of the bad-debt problem. Instead the preferred course has been to try to hide it in the hope that the problem will eventually correct itself. It should be noted that this is the exact opposite of the American strategy in dealing with banks' bad debts, most of them property-related, during the early 1990s. American banks were encouraged and even compelled by regulators, burned by the savings and loan mess, to reserve aggressively against their questionable property loans as soon as possible in a proactive attempt to force banks to recognize reality and start working their way out of their problems. This approach has worked remarkably well considering the scale of the problem. Wall Street has rewarded those banks that moved most decisively in this direction. In Japan, a country that culturally prefers the opaque over the transparent, there has been no such initiative. Instead there is a continuing collective attempt to pretend the losses never happened.

Consequently, a big, formal taxpayer-financed bailout of Japan's debt-beleaguered banking system remains unlikely. Or so at least hopes the Finance Ministry. Instead the planned way of dealing with the problem will involve, so long as the Finance Ministry succeeds in its sneaky aim, a continuing form of surreptitious taxpayer bailout that the ordinary Japanese citizen may never know about. The bailout is primarily taking the form of debt restructurings where bank lenders reduce the interest rate charged to troubled lenders to the level of the official discount rate (1.75 percent by September 1993) or ever lower, and therefore below the cost of what the banks themselves pay for funding. This is not quite as painful for banks' operating profits as might be thought because the Finance Ministry agreed in late 1992 to let banks subtract from their taxable income the difference between the interest received on such concessionary loans and the cost to the banks of funding them. This tax break supposedly applies so long as the interest rate concessions are considered essential or deemed "socially relevant." Previously the tax regime was onerous for banks in such cases. Interest rate concessions were viewed as charitable donations and banks were taxed on the interest originally due them even if they never received it. This tax concession is important given the strict tax regime in Japan when it comes to loan-loss write-offs and additions to bad debt reserves, the conventional ways of dealing with dud loans in the West. Certainly, the growing popularity of deals involving interest rate concessions, as the least bad of a variety of unpalatable alternatives, has become clear. Bank of Japan data show that loans at the ODR or less were growing in early 1993 at a rate of 50 percent per annum though admittedly from a very low base. By contrast, total bank loans were barely growing at all.

Clearly there can be no guarantee that the principal amount owed will ever be recovered in full in the case of borrowers for whom interest rate concessions are granted. Still, the Finance Ministry is fully behind this strategy despite the obvious risks. Its intentions are clear. First and foremost, it wants to buy time in the hope that over, say, a ten-year period the debt problem will right itself, thanks to a combination of inflation and economic growth. Second, to encourage banks to write loans off would quickly unmask glaring qualitative differences among Japanese banks. For some banks like Mitsubishi Bank have the financial means to afford such a house-cleaning strategy, whereas others, such as Nippon Credit Bank or Mitsui Trust, would risk insolvency if they followed this course. The result would be to shed a degree of light on the differing credit quality of Japanese banks, which the Finance Ministry would be most unhappy about. The mandarins dislike in principle the idea of conspicuous winners and losers in the supposedly deregulated banking industry over which they preside. Far better the traditional convoy approach, which at least suggests they are still in charge. The unmasking of losers would also cause the public to focus more on the Finance Ministry's own responsibility for the mess, which has occurred on its own turf.

For similar reason of cover-up it was always naive to expect to learn much when the banks disclosed for the first time ever their level of bad debts at the same time as they announced their final results for the financial year that ended in March 1993. For their discretion as to what to report was deliberately made immense. Bad debts were defined for this purpose as loans to bankrupt companies or loans on which interest had not been paid for six months. But banks did not have to include loans on which interest-rate concessions had been granted nor loans sold to the Soviet-sounding Cooperative Credit Purchasing Corporation. This was the recently established bank-owned loan liquidation vehicle where banks buy their own distressed loans with their own money and pay themselves interest. The only merit in this fudging exercise for the banks, aside from not having to report as bad the loans thus "sold," was to be able to deduct for tax purposes any loss incurred selling loans to the loan liquidation company at a discount to their face value. This was worth to the banks an estimated ¥100 billion in tax losses in the year that ended in March 1993. The aim of this warehousing exercise is again clear: to prevent loan write-offs and dumping of real estate collateral in the hope that the passage of time and inflation will eventually cause the problem to go away. Meanwhile, the Cooperative Credit Purchasing Corporation was to buy loans and not property itself, unlike the land-buying company originally proposed by the Finance Ministry in the autumn of 1992 in the heat of the stock market crisis, because there were too many unresolved disputes about which lender had first claim on collateral sometimes pledged many times over. The company was also to be financed by the banks themselves and not by the government, as originally proposed, because the politicians dared not admit to the public the need for a tax-payer bailout.

Such is Japan's strategy for dealing with its deluge of bad debts. Note also one broad macroeconomic problem with it. Japanese banks have been given every incentive, via the tax deductions offered on concessionary lending, to keep financing deadbeat creditors. Whereas a policy of encouraging more aggressive reserving against dud loans would enable banks to relend funds thus freed up to healthier firms that can better contribute to renewed economic growth. That the former activity is occurring is clear from a marked increase in lending to still distressed areas such as property. Thus, outstanding loans by Japan's big commercial banks (known as city banks) to the property sector increased by 8.8 percent in the year to March 1993. This hardly seems healthy at a time when city banks' total lending during the same period grew by just 0.3 percent.

The city banks as a group are probably the healthiest among Japan's different sorts of banks. Yet they will continue to write off and provide against lots of doubtful debts for several years to come. So the outlook for them remains boring at best. Yet such continued tedium depends on two cozy assumptions. The first is that the stock market does not collapse again, wiping out banks' remaining unrealized share gains, which is their main cushion against bad loans. Second, that the banks' bad-debt problems are under control in the sense that they are no longer rising. This is far from certain. A continuing weak economy, aggravated by the strength of the yen, will increase the volume of dud loans. The bulk of the existing bad loans stem from the speculative frenzy of the late 1980s and are mostly linked to real estate in some form or other. However, banks by the middle of 1993 were beginning to admit that an increasing number of loans were becoming nonperforming because of general economic weakness aggravated by the rise in the yen. Examples are small manufacturing concerns heavily dependent on exporting. This trend will also mean growing credit problems for some regional banks that, tucked away in more sober parts of the country, had managed to escape the worst of Tokyo's and Osaka's Bubble era excesses.

If "boring at best" is the most positive outlook for the banking sector, there remain many nooks and crannies in the compartmentalized world of Japanese finance that do not bear close scrutiny. One of the ugliest is the inaptly named trust banks. Japan's seven trust banks really consist of two institutions lodged under the same roof. That is, a commercial bank that takes in deposits and lends money on, and a trust business that invests assets held in trust on behalf of investors. These assets do not belong to the trust bank itself and therefore do not feature in the bank's balance sheet. Yet both types of business share one attribute. They have long-standing ties with the property business. Trust banks are the only Japanese banks that are allowed to act as real estate brokers. They also manage property held in trust. Unfortunately, these long-standing ties to the property world are reflected in trust banks' loan portfolios, both in the bank and the trust accounts. Loans to the property, construction and "finance" (for which read nonbanks) sectors accounted for 26 percent of trust banks' total bank assets at the end of September 1992. The exposure to these three problem sectors was even greater in the trust account at a huge 43 percent. Worse, most of these loans appear to have been made in the second half of the 1980s, since the incremental increase in the trust banks' lending during this period almost corresponds exactly with their current exposure to the construction, property and nonbank sectors. Logically, it might be assumed that since the assets held in the trust account do not feature on the banks' balance sheets they do not represent a credit risk to the bank. Logical perhaps but also wrong. The biggest source of funding for the trust side of the trust banks' business are so-called loan trusts and money trusts. There was a total of ￥55.5 trillion in loan trusts and ￥42.6 trillion in money trusts at the end of September 1992. These two products are essentially deposits of up to five years' maturity sold to individuals where the interest rate moves broadly in line with the government bond market. However, they are not technically nor legally bank deposits since they are held in trust and the trust bank is, strictly speaking, just managing the money on behalf of individual savers. This means that individuals who put their money in loan trusts and money trusts are not covered by Japan's limited deposit insurance system. But that does not help the trust banks in the event of a problem. For they are legally responsible for guaranteeing the principal invested in loan trusts and money trusts. Yet much of this money has been lent to the property, construction and nonbank sectors, while the reserves set aside against disaster are puny. Take Yasuda Trust, for example. It had ￥727 billion in its money trusts at the end of March 1990. The reserve then set aside for possible losses was a mere ￥1.1 billion.

The problem is so serious because the scale of the lending has been so great. Assets held in the trust account may only feature as a footnote in the trust banks' accounts. But they are very large. Mitsui Trust's trust assets are twice as large as its bank assets, and those of Chuo Trust, perhaps the sickest of the trust banks, are three times as large. The level of credit risk is therefore enormous. The total value of loans to the property, construction and nonbank sectors in the seven banks' trust accounts was ￥14.5 trillion at the end of September 1992. Trust banks then had between them ￥3.5 trillion of shareholders' equity plus ￥5.4 trillion of unrealized gains on their long-term shareholdings. That is not much of a cushion considering how many of these loans could turn out to be bad. And this was even before taking into account the ¥8.8 trillion of loans made to the same three problem sectors via the trust banks' ordinary banking business. No wonder more informed people in Tokyo have for some time assumed that many of the trust banks are technically insolvent.

If many credit problems remain concealed there are also problems dealing with those that are recognized disasters. For Japan is finding out that in such cases consensus, however desirable a goal, can be hard to achieve when financial interests do not coincide. This has certainly proved the case with rescheduling the debts of Japan's eight housing loan companies. Politically, this has so far been the hot potato of Japan's bad-debt crisis. These housing loan companies were set up in 1971 with banks acting as the founder shareholders. Their function was to advance mortgage loans to individuals as specialist mortgage lenders. But the housing loan companies diversified in the 1980s into financing property development, partly because of growing competition from banks themselves in the home loan business and partly because it was just the fashionable thing to do. The results were unusually disastrous even by post-Bubble standards. The eight housing loan companies had total loans at the end of 1992 of ¥14.4 trillion, of which nearly ¥6 trillion were bad. Seven of the eight have since been involved in extensive debt restructuring talks.

There are two political aspects to this problem, both of which have assured that the plight of these institutions has attracted more public attention than other seemingly more arcane areas of the financial services industry. First, Japan's cash-strapped but politically powerful agricultural financial cooperatives—in which Japan's electorally overrepresented farmers deposit their spare cash—are heavily exposed. Agricultural credit co-ops had lent the housing loan companies ¥3.8 trillion at the end of 1992, agricultural insurance co-ops had lent ¥1.4 trillion, and the obsessively secretive Norin-chukin, which acts as a central bank for the agricultural co-ops, had lent another ¥1.1 trillion. Clearly, it would be political dynamite if any agricultural co-ops went bust because of this lending. The banks' founding shareholders are the other major lenders to the housing loan companies.

The fact of the agricultural co-ops' exposure is bad enough. But perhaps worse from the point of view of orga-nizing a rescheduling has been their unhelpful attitude when presented with the prospect of suffering a loss. For the agri-cultural co-ops have argued that they only became involved in this mess because the Finance Ministry asked them, via the Ministry for Agriculture, Forestry and Fisheries, to support the housing loan companies by lending to them. They also have argued that they lent on the assumption that the found-ing banks' shareholders stood behind the loans. This is per-haps not so implausible since the agricultural co-ops did much of their lending to the housing loan companies at the tail end of the Bubble after (and also perhaps because) credit controls had already been imposed by the Finance Ministry on the banks' direct lending to property companies.

Such claims if true would certainly add to the already considerable embarrassment of the Finance Ministry. For it was instrumental in setting up the housing loan companies in the first place and several of its former senior officials occupy top positions at the eight companies, just as they do at most other major financial institutions. It has even been whispered that the agricultural co-ops threatened to link any agreement to a bailout plan with the vexed issue of opening up Japan's rice market. In other words, the farmers would only agree to the then still banned importing of rice into Japan if they could walk away from the losses incurred by their lending to the housing loan companies. That would mean encumbering the banks with an additional more than ¥5 trillion worth of non-performing debt on top of all their existing problems.

•

The second political problem is that the housing loan companies issued mortgage certificates that were mainly bought by small investors. These have no form of government guarantee attached to them. They are also much riskier than American-style mortgage-backed securities since they tend to be collateralized by a single property as opposed to a diversified pool of mortgages as is the case in the United States, and as such are another example of the antediluvian nature of Japanese finance. There also is no active secondary market in these certificates in Japan. Yet there were ¥10.8 trillion worth of mortgage certificates outstanding at the end of 1992, according to the Japan Mortgage Securities Association. Nippon Housing Loan, the biggest housing loan company, had issued some ¥200 billion worth. At the height of the boom it had brand-named this then hot-selling product *yorokobi*, which means "joy"!

The rescheduling of Nippon Housing Loan's debts was the first to be addressed. As the largest of the housing loan companies its case will probably serve as a precedent for the others, which is why the discussions were so contentious. The talks dragged on for months. In Nippon Housing Loan's case, the three largest founding city banks, Sanwa, Sakura and Daiwa, were asked to forgo all interest on their outstanding loans. The other six founding banks were asked to reduce their interest rate charge to 1.5 percent or lower. And all nine banks became jointly responsible for the outstanding mortgage certificates that had been issued. By contrast, Norinchukin was only asked to cut its interest rate to 2.5 percent while the agricultural co-ops would continue to receive 4.5 percent. These terms were set at a time when the ODR was still at 2.5 percent. The banks naturally, though unsuccessfully, tried to resist these terms. They were also concerned about putting their *hanko,* or seal, on any rescheduling documents lest that might make them responsible for the housing loan companies' total debts, including that of the agricultural credit co-ops. The bankers' concerns were legitimate, for this touchy core issue remained unaddressed. For if there were difficulties in seeking to agree on interest, how more tricky would it be negotiating a deal on the principal owed.

Meanwhile, the collateral underpinning all these loans has continued to depreciate in value. Unlike the rigged stock market, the property market has seen no recovery. Rather the reverse. Prices have continued to fall. As a result, Japan continues to suffer from the adverse consequences of its land-based monetary system, the so-called land standard, which allowed astronomic theoretical land values to be turned into instant credit during the Bubble years. Note that about 80 percent of a value of a property in Japan lies in the land, not the building.

Mitsui Fudosan is probably Japan's best-run property company. It published a slick brochure in early 1993 titled "Investing in Commercial Real Estate in Tokyo." The report sought naturally to cast the best light on a horrid situation. However, the authors in their eagerness to talk up the economy, and by direct implication the property market, resorted to an unfortunate analogy. "Japan's economy is nothing if not resilient. Like the Liberal Democratic Party, which has stayed in power ever since it was founded in 1955, the Japanese economy too has endured numerous challenges to its stability." The report then went on to refer hopefully to a post-Bubble "adjustment period" in both the property market and the economy. Adjustment, however, is a massive understatement for the scale of losses that have been sustained. The only reason there has not been more focus on this is because the property market is so illiquid. Yet values have continued to collapse on a breathtaking scale.

A rare glimpse of the real conditions on the ground was provided in a June 1993 report published by K.K. Halifax, a foreign-owned but Tokyo-based property consulting and development firm. This report analyzes the large amount of new buildings still coming on stream and concluded that the Tokyo office market would not bottom out until early 1996, by which time the vacancy rate in the twenty-three central wards of the capital city would hit 16 percent. This compared with an official vacancy rate in 1990 of less than 1 percent. To put this astonishing deterioration in some context, the report said that by 1995 the vacant space in central Tokyo will represent three times the amount of total office space in Seattle's central business district and almost double Boston's total stock of office space. This looming surge in empty office space is despite project cancellations. Thus, the massive 1980s-style ¥10 trillion Tokyo Bay development project has been put on ice, a victim of the market slump. This proposed high-tech city, combining new office buildings and luxury apartments on six kilometers of reclaimed land south of the prime Ginza district, is now unlikely to be completed until well into the twenty-first century.

Genuine arm's-length transactions in the commercial property market remain few and far between because no one, least of all the banks, has any interest in seeing the true value of pledged collateral exposed on a marked-to-market basis. But a rare glimpse at reality was provided by a deal concluded at the end of May 1993. A nine-story building in the best area of the Ginza was sold for ¥59 million per *tsubo* (roughly, three square meters). This was almost half the National Land Agency's ¥113.8 million official estimate of the value of land in this section of the Ginza.

However, it is the meltdown in Tokyo's office rental market that provides the best picture of just how sick the overall property market remains. The decline has been both dramatic and sudden not only because the property market has fallen but also because rental leases in Japan are readily renegotiable. Consequently, Tokyo now has one of the most liquid office rental markets in the world (in stark contrast to the still almost complete lack of genuine arm's-length sale transactions). In many major office markets long-term rental leases are signed for up to fifteen to twenty-five years, as is the case in London, or at least for five years as is more standard in New York. And if a lease is broken a tenant is obliged to pay back some negotiated discount of the rental stream still owed. However, in Tokyo leases can be canceled at any time subject to only six months' notice. This has not been a problem for landlords in living memory, since the market has always been so tight with near zero vacancy rates. So rents have always risen. No longer. Three years ago it was accepted wisdom that rents could never fall because, after all, Tokyo, as the Mitsui Fudosan report earnestly chronicles, is the world's "most populous city," where more than 25 percent of Japan's entire population is concentrated in the greater Tokyo region, an area that occupies a mere 3.6 percent of Japan's total land area. The speciousness of such conventional arguments is now grimly apparent. Tokyo office rents by 1993 were 60 percent down from their early 1991 peak. The downward adjustment has been so fast and so extreme precisely because tenants can threaten to walk, as many have done when landlords have not promptly agreed to lower rentals to market-clearing levels. With office rentals the second biggest cost item for most companies operating in Japan after personnel, both foreign and Japanese companies have been increasingly willing to test the market. While stunned landlords have discovered to their horror that the way the leases are drawn up massively favors the tenants.

By the summer of 1993 Tokyo was abuzz with stories about the fantastic deals that had been cut. American investment bank Salomon Brothers, for example, threatened to move from all of the three floors it occupies of NTT's flashy Urbannet Otemachi Building in the heart of Tokyo's financial district, which opened in 1990 and which has been nicknamed the "Bubble Building" as a symbol of bull market excess. As a result, Salomon is reckoned to have lowered its rental cost from around ¥85,000 per *tsubo* to roughly half that figure. Salomon will not confirm the exact details. The firm anyway gave up one floor, and NTT, in a departure from normal practice, agreed to pay the considerable cost of making good the space vacated. Salomon was definitely prepared to move if necessary, since it was offered space in Shiroyama Hills at a rate of only around ¥35,000 per *tsubo*. This is a 95,000-square-meter building located behind Tokyo's smart Hotel Okura and jointly owned by Mori Building, a large unquoted property company, and Japan Tobacco. Mori has been among the smarter of Tokyo's major landlords. Recognizing reality, it has lowered rents to clearing levels to make sure its buildings remain occupied and cash flow keeps coming in. Mitsubishi Estate, however, has not. True, it announced that rentals for new tenants in Marunouchi, Tokyo's prime office district where Mitsubishi Estate is the dominant landlord, would not be increased in 1993 by the usual 5 percent over the ¥89,000 per *tsubo* asked in 1992. Still, even that reduced figure was way above the market. Consequently, Mitsubishi has begun to lose tenants to other buildings in Marunouchi as well as other areas. The word among its tenants was that by the summer of 1993 it had begun to panic about the prospect of unwanted empty space. Russell Reynolds, a headhunting firm, rented space in June 1993 in the Taisho Seimei building in Marunouchi for only ¥45,000 per *tsubo*. Only the previous summer when the same building was opened, the landlord began trying to rent the space at ¥75,000 per *tsubo*. In less-central areas of Tokyo's twenty-three wards space in new buildings is now on offer at less than ¥20,000 per *tsubo*.

These individual examples are worth quoting in some detail since the collapse in rentals is the best indication of the plunge in Japanese land values. For ultimately the only safe way of valuing a piece of property is in terms of the income that can be generated from it, an elementary lesson the Japanese have only just learned. This is why a 60 percent decline in office rentals is also an accurate reflection of at least a similar decline in commercial property values. This implies a dramatic loss of wealth as well as a drastic depreciation of the value of collateral underpinning the rickety banking system. And it has taken place before any deregulation of the land market, which, by increasing the supply of housing, would cause a further decline in property values.

This explains why, more than any other country in the early 1990s, Japan will suffer the capitalist world's worst bout of asset deflation. For it has so much debt collateralized against property values that may not be seen again for another twenty years or longer. This is a mighty large hole that it will take a long time to crawl out of. Nor will trade partners be forgiving. For though the Japanese will continue to try to pretend that the losses in their own domestic property market never happened, Japanese investors, or rather the banks that lent to them, will increasingly liquidate their property investments held overseas, where they have also suffered huge losses, though (in yen terms) not nearly so large as the losses within Japan. They will do so to raise badly needed cash. This will prompt legitimate charges that the Japanese are exporting their domestic real estate distress since they do not want to knock their own market by dumping assets in Japan. Still, such overseas sales will represent great bargains for the buyers. An example occurred in September 1993 when a subsidiary of Hilton Hotels bought a Hawaii hotel for only 25 percent of the 1980s construction cost from a group of Japanese bank lenders led by Mitsubishi Bank. The 1,241-room sixty-one-acre Hyatt Regency Wakoloa resort hotel on the island of Hawaii only opened for business in 1988. It was part of the nearly $10 billion that Japanese investors plowed into Hawaii hotels between 1985 and 1990 in yet another *folie de grandeur*. It will be a long time before such madness is repeated.

But in the meantime the hangover from the 1980s' spending binge has spread into the industrial sphere. The resulting challenge will produce as big a sea change in the way Japanese manufacturers go about their business as the bursting of the Bubble has already done for the banks and brokers.

5

Auto Industry—The Titans Are No Longer

DURING THE 1980s it was assumed by expert and laymen alike that the Japanese carmakers would conquer the world motor industry. The only point at issue was how long this seemingly unstoppable process would take. Such a deterministic view holds sway no longer. When Nissan, the country's second largest carmaker, announced in February 1993 the first closure of a Japanese car plant since the Second World War, it was taken as symbolic proof that the mighty industry, which still accounts for about three quarters of Japan's trade surplus with the United States and which for so long has been the hallmark of Japanese manufacturing excellence, was finally having to slam on the brakes. Retrenchment has indeed become the order of the day. This matters because a downturn for the carmakers deepens the economic gloom for everyone else. The Japanese motor industry, including parts suppliers, employs 10 percent of the country's industrial workers and accounts for fully 13 percent of its manufacturing output. It therefore represents the guts of the economy that created the Japanese miracle.

When the Bubble first burst the carmakers thought, or rather, hoped, that they were suffering from merely a normal cyclical slowdown. Domestic car sales have been falling since

September 1990 but the true extent of their predicament only began to dawn on senior management about halfway through 1992. In reality the industry, which has until now only really ever experienced an increase in its production volumes, faces nothing less than its biggest challenge since its inception. The Japanese carmakers realize belatedly that they have created far too much manufacturing capacity in high-cost Japan, that their major export markets are mature and cannot bail them out of the recessionary doldrums at home, and that in some notable cases their rivals have become significantly more competitive. This does not mean that the Japanese motor industry is doomed to decline from here on. For those carmakers that act quickly enough and boldly enough to reduce their costs should continue as tomorrow's winners. But not all will survive. For the Japanese auto industry, as for many others, this unnerving and unprecedented challenge means transforming their business by putting profits ahead of the traditional race for market share. The market share strategy is dead because the Japanese firms' global shares are unlikely to increase in the future from their recent peak. This consideration, combined with mounting financial constraints, means turning the business on its head by addressing the cost issue first to shore up operating profitability and then letting sales take care of themselves.

The problems are by now clear enough. The motor industry suffered its third consecutive year of declining earnings in the financial year that ended in March 1993. Many carmakers are already losing money, most notably Nissan. It lost ¥26 billion at the present level that fiscal year while its sales fell by 8 percent. Mazda is also in the red and could lose ¥40 billion in the year to March 1994. While even Toyota, Japan's biggest producer and the pioneer of the "lean production" system that changed seemingly forever the way cars are built, has felt the pain. Toyota's net profit declined by 45 percent to ¥238 billion in the year to June 1992, which is the month when its financial year ends. That was still more profit than any other Japanese company reported that year. But two thirds of Toyota's earnings came from interest income on its cash hoard and dividends received on its shareholdings in other firms, not from carmaking. Even more telling, the carmaker's operating margins (i.e., the profitability of its primary business of selling cars) collapsed from 4 percent to 1.4 percent.

The rapid rise of the yen since then has only compounded Toyota's and the rest of the industry's woes. The other Japanese carmakers' operating margins, excluding Toyota, are already below 1 percent. These are the lowest profit margins since the war. And if the yen remains strong it seems only a matter of time before the whole industry is in a loss. Toyota made this abundantly plain when it announced its final results for its financial year, which ended in June 1993. These showed a further 26 percent decline in net profits on flat sales. Ryuji Araki, general manager of Toyota's financial division, used the occasion to warn publicly that if the yen stayed above the ¥110 level to the dollar for the forthcoming financial year, then Toyota could suffer its first ever operating loss since it was founded in 1937. He added, in case anyone failed to get the message, that the company faced potentially the most serious crisis in its history. Toyota is not a company known for giving away lots of information to the press, so the point behind Araki's public remarks was obvious. It was to make crystal clear to government policy makers, be they bureaucrats or politicians, the threat the rising yen posed to Japan's domestic manufacturing base and therefore to the stability of the employment system.

This is dramatic stuff since the Japanese carmakers as a group have never been in the red. Yet such records are there to be broken. The carmakers have seen an unprecedented post-Bubble collapse in domestic sales in their home market. New vehicle sales peaked at 6 million in 1990. They were 5.3

million in 1992 and 4.9 million in 1993. The main reason is depressed consumer spending in an economy where disposable income is growing by barely 2 percent a year. Carmakers hope fondly that their customers will return to their old habit of replacing their cars every four years. But in the present frugal climate it is more likely they will stick with what they have after paying off the installment financing. About half the cars sold in Japan are bought with bank financing. This signals continuing cuts in production ahead. Car production was down by 13.5 percent in January 1993, compared with the same month the previous year. Six months later and the trend was still weakening. Toyota's domestic production was down 15.2 percent in the year to July while exports, savaged by the soaring yen, were down 12.6 percent over the same period.

The collapse in production has drawn attention to the excessive investment undertaken during the 1980s, some of which may well end up being mothballed. Toyota, Nissan and Mazda, for example, committed nearly $3 billion to the construction of four newly automated assembly plants in Japan, all of which opened in the early 1990s. Yet at the start of 1993 none of these plants was operating at full capacity. Nissan's decision to close its twenty-nine-year-old Zama factory near Tokyo by early 1995 will barely put a dent in this excessive capacity. But the closure will mean the loss of five thousand jobs, or nearly one tenth of the firm's workforce in Japan. The firm has said the jobs will go by natural attrition. This may all seem fairly undramatic stuff compared with the scores of car and components factories shut down in America and Europe in the past decade. Even Germany's Daimler-Benz has said it will lay off a total of eighty thousand employees in 1993 and 1994. But by Japanese standards the bald announcement of a factory closure was considered a major event and was treated as such by the local media.

More such closures will be needed if the Japanese motor industry is to remain competitive. The post-Bubble plunge in

THE END OF JAPAN INC.

car sales has caught the Japanese industry on the hop. For the traditional answer to previous downturns in the domestic market no longer applies: there is no major growth market for the Japanese to export their surplus cars to. Japanese car exports to the United States peaked at 2.35 million in 1986. They will have been around 1.4 million in 1993. True, in America, car sales have begun to grow again but the Japanese have started to lose market share there. On top of this the Japanese producers need to utilize the capacity of the so-called transplant factories that most of them opened in the United States during the 1980s. The capacity of these plants is already more than 2 million a year and therefore near to the level of Japan's nearly 30 percent share of the American market of around 8 million cars. Cars made at transplants have even begun to be exported back to Japan. Then there is the trade issue. The car industry represents by far the biggest slice of America's trade deficit with Japan. America's deficit with Japan in cars and car parts has been running at more than $30 billion annually. Clearly, any rise in Japanese car-related imports into America would be bound to attract flak or worse from the Clinton administration. And besides, car exports are still limited by a voluntary-restraint agreement first signed back in 1981, whose continued existence is proof of the enduring unofficial reality of managed-trade arrangements.

If America offers limited growth so does Europe. Here the key production center is Britain, which has been selected as the Trojan horse for Japan's entry into the European Community's car market. The plan is that by the end of 1994 Japanese transplants will account for 50 percent of Britain's total production capacity of 2 million cars compared with total sales in the British market in 1992 of only 1.6 million. The recently opened British factories of Toyota, Honda and Nissan have been geared up for an export drive into mainland Europe. Yet the timing has been unfortunate. European car sales have been plummeting under the deflationary yoke of the Bundesbank-linked European Monetary System, while the Japanese carmakers' share of a declining market will be limited by an as-yet-to-be-finalized agreement with the European Commission. The arbitrary terms are still in dispute precisely because the weakness of demand for new cars in Europe has far surpassed too sanguine expectations. But the Japanese will probably have to agree to a least a 10 percent decline in their exports from the previous year's level in a European car market that may have suffered a nearly 20 percent decline in sales in 1993. It is true that longer term the rest of Asia offers tremendous potential in view of the low levels of car ownership, especially in a vast country like China. But much of that potential remains several years away while the downturn plaguing the industry is here today. Southeast Asia still accounts for only 10 percent of the Japanese motor industry's exports.

With no export market then to bail them out of their current problems at home the carmakers have begun to do the next obvious thing. That is to address their bloated costs. For the slump in sales has coincided with a dramatic rise in the industry's break-even point, the result of escalating costs. One reason for this has been the need to pay, in the form of higher depreciation charges, for all that capital investment undertaken in recent years. The motor industry spent ¥6.1 trillion in the five years to March 1992 building new plants and modernizing old ones. The result is chronic domestic production overcapacity of at least 50 percent based on total capacity of 10 million and total sales (domestic, 2.5 million and export, 2 million) of less than 5 million. These estimates are not as alarmist as many will suppose.

Another problem, noted by Steve Usher, a Tokyo-based analyst at the British securities firm Kleinwort Benson, has been a huge surge in spending on parts and raw materials. The main reason for this was the Japanese carmakers' obsession with product proliferation. Helped by their famed manufacturing flexibility, the carmakers sought to cater to every conceivable consumer whim. Thus, one Nissan model offered eighty-six different types of steering wheel. Toyota provided thirty-two types of sound systems in the cars it exported to America. While Nippondenso, a major components producer, supplied more than five hundred different kinds of air conditioners to Toyota alone. As a consequence, the proportion of costs attributed to parts and raw materials had soared to 72 percent by March 1992, up from 63 percent in March 1983.

Curiously, the final assemblers' profit margins have been under pressure while the components industry has enjoyed relatively stable profit margins, the result of the demand for all those different sorts of parts. This will not last though. The rationalization of the components industry has now become the total priority of the carmakers, following a path that has already been well trodden by their Detroit-based competitors. Yoshifumi Tsuji, president of Nissan, views reducing the sums spent on components as the most important aspect of his firm's present cost-cutting drive. About 75 percent of Nissan's manufacturing costs are now accounted for by parts brought in from outside suppliers, he said in a 1993 interview.

The Japanese now realize they went far too far in the drive for diversity of product lines, a case of flexible manufacturing being taken to its logical though ultimately silly extreme by overenthusiastic engineers. Take again the example of Nissan. Speaking in April 1993, Tsuji, himself an engineer and manufacturing expert, remarked: "Only two to three years ago there was a tendency to believe that small-lot production was the only way to meet customers' needs. Now we realize that there is no such need." This is a remarkable admission. The by now abandoned obsession with product proliferation is also a classic example of the tendency for Japanese companies in the same industrial sector all to pursue the same goal and all to switch course at the same time. The result is that no one company ever gains a permanent competitive advantage since they are all following one another's strategy.

There is now an industry-wide drive within the Japanese motor industry both to standardize components and to reduce the number of models on offer. The internal word went out at Nissan in May 1992 when employees received an announcement from senior management of the urgent need to change course. A special committee was formed under Tsuji's leadership. This then divided into three subcommittees to concentrate on three separate but related tasks: a reduction in the number of models, a reduction in the number of parts, and an evaluation committee to monitor the actions taken by the two other committees. About 250 parts were selected, the number of different kinds of which had to be reduced by 40 percent. This goal had been reached in many cases by mid-1993, as had a targeted 40% reduction in the number of models Nissan sells. Joint procurement among carmakers is also on the rise, although from a low base, as are mergers among component firms belonging to the same industrial group. Nissan and Mazda are engaged in joint procurement of transmissions while Toyota has begun to purchase a portion of its seat supply from a Nissan producer, Tachi-S. Still, so far collaboration remains relatively small outside *keiretsu* groups. The carmakers have been keen competitors for too long to forget old habits. Still, it is a sign of how bad conditions have become that this is happening at all.

An extreme example of what had been occurring in terms of the excesses of parts proliferation is combination meters. The combination meter, a part of the display panel, provides an interesting microcosm of the motor industry as a whole. Hidehiko Yashiro, a senior engineer in the electronics design section at the Nissan Technical Center located an hour's drive from Tokyo, is a specialist in this niche area. Yashiro tells how for at least five years before action was finally taken, the designers' department had continually been making requests to the product planning department to reduce the number of different kinds of combination meters used. The request was made because the greater the number of different kinds of the same part required, the more design drawings which had to be prepared and the more space required to store all these different sorts of parts at the assembly plant. This was viewed by the designers as impractical, wasteful and also unnecessary effort. The same experience was repeated with other types of components. Yashiro says: "We have argued for quite a long time to reduce the number of parts but we were not able to convince the product planning people that there were too many parts. There was a basic idea that the more variety of products the better the customer would like it." Yet the customers' response showed that this was not the case. Thus, the Nissan Technical Center released sixty-five variations of the Sunny B13 steering wheel when that then new model went into production in 1990. But in the four-month period from June 1991 to October 1991 orders for 95 percent of the thirty thousand cars produced each month were covered by just twenty types of steering wheel. The other forty-five were hardly ever ordered. Despite such clear evidence, it proved impossible to persuade the product planning people to depart from conventional practice until the official order to change policy came down from senior management on high. Meanwhile the design people never talked to the marketing people, a dialogue that may have produced a change in policy earlier, because the existence of the product planning function effectively blocked communication between these two areas. So much for Japan's famed management by consultation and dialogue with the employees. Still, the lesson has now been learned. There will be only seventy types of combination meter in the next model of the Sunny B13, which will be launched in early 1994. There used to be 437.

It is true that as the highest cost producer among the top firms and burdened with a lot of debt, Nissan has embarked on probably the most aggressive cost cutting to date because it has had the biggest financial scare. Its corporate goal is to reduce the variety of parts it uses by 40 percent over three years beginning in 1993, and eventually the number of different variations of models it offers by 50 percent. Both Mazda and Toyota plan cuts of 30 percent in both areas. Nissan reckons its retrenchment will cut its purchasing budget, in terms of the amount spent on materials and components, by ¥100 billion over a three-year period. This task will involve significant reengineering of models as well as the cooperation of suppliers. The firm hopes to cut another ¥100 billion from its costs by a combination of a reduction in labor expenses (¥25 billion), a standardization of parts (¥30 billion) and increased productivity and other miscellaneous savings (¥45 billion). But even further action could be required. Take the product development cycle. Most Japanese carmakers would gladly replace their models once every five or six years instead of the present four-year norm. Indeed many have begun to follow this course. This will have the benefit of extending depreciation periods and concentrating more employees' time on fewer products. Toyota has so far refused to join this trend, however. Still, even it as market leader is not likely to hold out for too long since the savings are simply too significant. The word within the motor industry is that Toyota has already begun to consider lengthening its own product cycles.

Another key variable is labor costs. So far every effort has been made to spread the pain by slashing bonuses and reducing the number of hours worked. This has already resulted in a significant decline in take-home pay for employees, since overtime accounts for about 10 percent of the average pay packet and bonuses for up to 30 percent. However, whether outright dismissals can be avoided remains extremely unlikely since there is simply no need to produce so many cars in high-cost Japan. Certainly, the desire for now not to be seen laying off workers remains strong, as is clear from the ultra-delicate way Nissan handled the closure of the Zama factory.

Sacking employees still gives a company a bad name in Japan, inhibiting its ability to recruit the best graduates in the future and even affecting sales of its products. Nissan certainly suffered a bigger drop in its sales in the domestic market than the rest of the auto industry following the headline coverage given by the Japanese press to its decision to shut Zama.

So the Japanese carmakers will try to hang on to the vestiges of their traditional system, such as lifetime employment. But it will be a hard act to pull off given the recent strength of the yen. The Japanese motor industry still has far higher foreign exchange revenues than foreign exchange costs, despite the growth in overseas production during the 1980s. Toyota is the most vulnerable of the majors in this respect since it assembles only 16 percent of its vehicles abroad compared with, for example, Honda's 33 percent. And every day the yen stays strong the greater the pain. One senior Nissan executive, speaking in the summer of 1993, remarked that if the yen stayed above ¥115 to the dollar for the next eighteen months his company would be forced in the interests of its sheer survival to close every factory in Japan. This may sound like an exaggeration. But it shows the pressures that are steadily building under the surface. One point is sure. If one major vehicle producer decides it can no longer avoid outright layoffs or plant closures in Japan and acts accordingly, its competitors will quickly follow, as will the chain of components suppliers, since the precedent will have been set. The only thing that has prevented more dramatic retrenchment action from being taken already is the employers' sense of social responsibility combined with fear of government disapproval or worse. This is not a matter of legality. It is a matter of example. The question is how long the carmakers can continue to grin and bear this situation. That in turn will depend, first, on how long it takes for the domestic market to recover and, second, on the level of the currency. In the meantime, the structure of the Japanese auto industry will change dramatically. Indeed, Nissan's financial plight may just prove a blessing in disguise by providing it with the boost needed to switch course most decisively—just as Ford's near bankruptcy in the early 1980s gave it a head start over then financially fat but still lumbering General Motors. As for Japan's other carmakers, even debt-less Toyota will soon have to follow the same course with more aggressive pruning. This will mean ruthlessly cutting costs to improve profitability in a 1990s world where the term "downsizing" has already become in America a management-consultant-speak cliché, just as "globalization" was the buzz word in the debt-financed expansion of the 1980s. Not all the companies will prove up to the challenge. It is almost certain that within a few years there will be many fewer than Japan's eleven current carmakers.

The scale of the long-term problems facing the Japanese motor industry were well signaled in a 1992 paper by Michael Smitka, a professor at Washington and Lee University in Virginia.* He argued persuasively that there is far too much car-making capacity in Japan and that most of it has become far less competitive than in the past. As a result, Japanese carmakers will be forced to cut both their capacity at home and their exports. If this turns out to be true, the world's greatest source of trade friction should gradually fade away. Japan's carmakers still in 1992 exported 45 percent of the cars made in their Japanese factories. This effort accounted for a huge 22 percent of Japan's total exports. In 1992 America's deficit with Japan on car trade accounted for about 75 percent of its total $44 billion bilateral trade deficit with Japan. But within ten years, predicts Smitka, America's deficit on cars will shrink to "insignificance." Japanese carmakers will shift more production to America, and their current 27 percent share of the American market (including cars made there) will drop to 22 percent.

* "The Decline of the Japanese Auto Industry."

All this seems eminently plausible. Indeed, the only question is perhaps whether the drop in Japan's market share will be even greater. Yet to most people Smitka's forecast will appear apocalyptically gloomy. Such conventional folk have not studied the huge loss of competitive advantage suffered by the Japanese, a deterioration only temporarily camouflaged by the exuberance of the late 1980s' Bubble. The first area is labor costs. In 1970 Japanese wages were only 38 percent of the American level. Such a competitive advantage is now ancient history. Wages in the Japanese motor industry, including parts makers as well as assemblers, have more than doubled in dollar terms since 1985. Smitka estimates that Japanese wages were $18.90 an hour in 1992 compared with $14.60 in America, though admittedly that gap narrows somewhat if the generous pensions and other benefits offered by Detroit's Big Three are included. Since then American wage rises have been minimal, reflecting the soft American economy, while Japanese wage rates, in dollar terms, have risen significantly, thanks to the rising yen and to an estimated $22 per hour based on the ¥111 per dollar exchange rate that prevailed in April 1993. The second loss of comparative advantage concerns cost of capital. The Tokyo stock market crash brought an end to the era of cheap capital, a big blow for capital-hungry businesses such as car making. Like other Japanese firms, carmakers will have to pay back huge sums raised through the sale of equity warrants that they once thought were going to be converted into shares. Nine Japanese carmakers issued a total of ¥820 billion bonds with warrants attached during the bull market that will now have to be refinanced. The extra cost of refinancing, assuming that money was not lost on stock market investments and similar misadventures, will further reduce cash reserves already under pressure from falling earnings or even outright losses. Even ultraconservative Toyota has felt the impact financially. It still retains a formidably strong balance sheet. Yet its holding of cash and securities, net of bond issues outstanding, has more than halved from the ¥ 12.2 trillion figure reached in 1990.

The third area where competitive advantage has been lost is in the manufacturing area. The just-in-time system was clearly taken too far by the Japanese carmakers in terms of the trend toward product proliferation, the result in the most part of engineers being allowed to run wild within these companies. Note that this is the opposite of Detroit's old affliction, where the Big Three were run by accountants who knew nothing about cars. Smitka writes: "Maintaining all these literally millions of separate parts in production magnifies the logistics, inventory and management problems of the entire industry." The just-in-time system has also run into the mundane practical obstacle of traffic congestion. This makes frequent deliveries increasingly different, especially in the Tokyo area. And in the Yokohama-Kawasaki area just outside Tokyo, for example, trucks have had to cut their daily deliveries from three to two. Also many plants, as in the case of Zama, are now comparatively old. They were originally built in underpopulated areas outside cities that have since become, thanks to rapid economic growth, busy dormitory towns. This not only increases the congestion. It also prevents expansion of existing manufacturing sites since in many cases the predominantly white-collar residents of these suburban neighborhoods no longer like the idea of having a car plant in their midst. And they certainly do not aspire to work in one. The affluent Japanese now shun this type of work, which is commonly referred to by the slogan the three K's—*kianai, kitsui* and *kiken*—meaning dirty, hard and dangerous. This explains why in recent years both Nissan and Toyota decided to set up new factories in the southern island of Kyushu where it is easier to build modern facilities from scratch. Another problem is that the quality of the workforce has deteriorated as the nature of the work becomes more undesirable. Smitka reckons the average age of a worker at most plants is approaching forty and at some factories half the workers are over age fifty. This has slowed the pace of production lines. And as bad, younger workers are not proving so loyal. Turnover rates among college graduates hired in April 1987 have reached nearly 30 percent. True, this problem will fade somewhat with the weaker economy since school leavers will be happy with whatever work they can find whereas during the Bubble boom the carmakers were forced to hire large numbers of temporary foreign workers just to keep the production lines moving. Still, the point is that traditional Japanese-style manufacturing is, at the very least, fraying at the edges.

Smitka's long-term forecast is that Japan's factories will not reach 1991's volume of output "before 1995 if ever," given the mounting costs of production. This again is not so extreme a forecast. Indeed, the signs of an end of an era of Japanese dominance in autos are fast emerging in the American market. This is best demonstrated by the experience of Honda, Japan's most "American" car manufacturer. The first Japanese company to set up an American production facility, Honda's Accord was the best-selling car in America from 1989 to 1991. But in the first three months of 1993 sales of the Accord collapsed by 40 percent with the car languishing ninth in the sales charts while Honda as a whole saw its market sales fall by 18 percent during the same period. In such an adverse climate Honda began to resort to the same brand-weakening tactics long employed by the Detroit producers, namely offering financial discounts to dealers to boost sales. Nor was Honda's experience unique. Toyota's sales declined by 7 percent in the same three-month period and Mazda's by 16 percent. In all, the Japanese carmakers experienced their worst sales performance in America since the late 1970s—the only exception was Nissan, which had a hit product in America in 1993 with the new Altima.

The Japanese firms' total market share (including cars

built in Japanese factories in America as well as those exported from Japan) sank to 27 percent in the first three months of 1993, compared with 30 percent the previous year. Hence growing talk that the Japanese share of the American car market has peaked. This development is partly the result of the American producers offering better-quality cars. But it also reflects the higher prices that the Japanese producers have had to charge to compensate for the rising yen, a tactic they have had to resort to increasingly since mid-1992 because there have been no domestic profits to subsidize their export operations. This has affected not only cars imported from Japan but also those Japanese cars "made" in America. Many of these are built using imported components from Japan, such as engines and transmissions. As a result, Japanese models are now often more expensive in the American market than equivalent American models. The same trend applies at the luxury end of Japan's product range. Since the car's launch in the autumn of 1989, the base price of Toyota's Lexus LS400 has increased from $35,000 to $45,000. This is not insignificant. But price is not the only issue, though it is a major one. For the cars made by American manufacturers have indeed improved substantially. After years of mouthing about the need for "quality," Detroit has finally begun to implement it relatively consistently. American consumers have evidently started to notice this, though it helps that Japanese cars are now on average nearly $2,500 more expensive than equivalent American models. The one advantage that the Japanese producers still have over Detroit is that they do not have to shoulder the high union benefit costs, such as health insurance, that the American producers do. This is the result of the much younger workforces at their American transplant factories. Still, it was a sign of changed times when hard-pressed Mazda sold in June 1992 fifty percent of its Flat Rock, Michigan, plant to Ford. Whatever the financial reasons for doing this it has made Mazda that much more vulnerable to currency movements, not to mention outright protectionism, since it is now that much more dependent on exporting.

In fact, more overseas production, not less, seems the only way for the Japanese carmakers to go—which makes Mazda's move seem even more bizarre. Toyota and Nissan each have six assembly plants in North America and Europe (including joint-venture facilities), and Honda has four. By contrast, Mazda has just half a plant in America and none in Europe. The level of Japanese overseas production seems bound to increase in the future, if only as a logical reaction to the soaring cost of manufacturing in Japan. Nissan's current split between exports and local production is 1:1. It expects that to have increased to 2:1 in favor of local production by the end of the 1990s. The trend may happen even quicker than that, though, so intense are the financial pressures. In August 1993 70 percent of Nissan vehicles sold in America were built in the United States, a monthly record. The following month Honda announced that by 1996 all the Civics and Accords it sells in America would be made in America. The same trend toward local production is evident in parts procurement. Nissan, for example, has increased the amount of components it buys in America from $2.3 billion to $3.7 billion between 1992 and 1994. This is all part of the hollowing-out thesis, whereby an increasing amount of Japanese production will be moved offshore. Quite how ominous such a development will be for those employed by the Japanese carmakers at home is of course another matter.

Much of this increase in overseas production by the Japanese carmakers will occur in Asia. They already have a dominant more than 80 percent share of the Southeast Asian vehicle market. The motor boom in these countries in recent years has been fueled primarily by demand for trucks and other sorts of commercial vehicles. By the second half of the 1990s full-scale motorization should have begun with an expanding middle class in countries like Thailand, Indonesia and the Philippines. And then there is China. All of this should mean more and more Japanese plants sited in Asia. A 1993 survey by Fourin, Inc., a Nagoya-based auto consultancy firm, estimated that by 1997 Japanese carmakers' overseas plants will be able to produce 6.7 million units, up from 5.3 million in 1993. Out of this total, production in China and Southeast Asia will expand during the same period from 790,000 vehicles to 2.3 million. It is therefore not surprising that by the middle of 1993 Nissan for one had begun active planning for a factory in China to be located in the Manchuria region. In fact, Fourin's figures may well prove to be an underestimate of the extent to which Japanese production will be driven offshore to other parts of Asia in coming years. The rate of change could prove rather dramatic with the key swing factor being the value of the yen. Speaking in April 1993 at a time when the yen was at 111 to the dollar (it was ¥101 four months later in August), Nissan's Tsuji said: "My largest worry is the rise in the yen." It was a comment that there was no reason to disbelieve. But far less credible was another point the Nissan president made almost simultaneously: "We don't need to dismiss any people."

That incredibly confident assertion will prove to have no grounding in reality, which is unfortunate for the social consensus that has persisted for so long in Japan. As unfortunate is that so much of Japan's industrial prowess, as reflected in its trade surplus, is accounted for by the motor industry. For this is the most mature of industries with saturated markets in all the world's industrialized countries. In the industries of tomorrow the Japanese are not positioned where you would expect them to be. That failure is one more example of the pressures that have led to the End of Japan Inc.

6

Computers, Electronics and Telecommunications— Left Far Behind

THEY CALLED IT "the Compaq shock" in Japan. The term refers to the devastating psychological impact on Japan's computer industry when America's Compaq toward the end of 1992 began to sell personal computers at half the list price of market leader, NEC. The event symbolized for the Japanese mass media two startling trends: first, just how uncompetitive the Japanese electronics industry had become; and, second, the resurgence of American business as a competitive force in the industry of the future. Yet barely five years previously the high-tech challenge posed by Japan was a subject of national preoccupation among policy makers in both America and Europe. Indeed, issues of national security were raised in this debate by an insidious lobby of closet protectionists and economic nationalists in Washington and the capitals of Europe. There was much lobbying of government for taxpayer funding to help companies respond to this perceived Japanese threat. Yet in the end this once fashionable cause célèbre, like so many other trendy enthusiasms, has proved to be way off the mark, if not total nonsense.

American companies remain at the pioneering vanguard of the high-tech revolution; the result of the remarkably vibrant entrepreneurial energy that still exists in the United

States despite the socialistic interventionist tendencies of the incumbent Clinton administration. This risk-taking ethic is combined with its natural counterpart, a dynamic venture capital industry. Japan, by contrast, barely has a venture capital industry. The country faces deep-seated problems in its computer industry, be it in the fields of hardware or software. Its famous consumer electronics makers have also run aground.

So, the brutal truth is that supposedly "high-tech" Japan is way behind America in the race to dominate what it is increasingly clear will be tomorrow's information economy. It is America that controls the technology and it is from American companies that other countries' companies have to buy it. This raises the larger question of whether the Japanese post-1945 economic miracle was merely a product of prowess in manufacturing, the ability to mass-produce goods; a skill that was naturally suited to Japan's national traits of social conformity and suppression from an early age of all forms of individualism. If so, Japan may not be expected to prosper to the same extent in an information age where the skills of creativity and adaptability will command a higher premium.

These may be sweeping generalizations. But they reflect concerns currently preoccupying Japanese policymakers. The increasingly evident failure of the Japanese in the computer area is certainly in stark contrast to the promise of so few years ago. It has raised basic questions about whether the traditional Japanese education system, with its emphasis on rote learning in contrast to the Western liberal arts tradition of cultivating critical judgment and an inquiring mind, are really the skills best suited to the needs of serving an information society. Producing an army of disciplined number crunchers may make sense in an order shaped by mass production techniques. But in tomorrow's world of knowledge workers, what will count is less the ability to process information, a task that will increasingly be borne by ever more user-friendly machines, than to know what to do with all that information or "noise" which the machines constantly spew out. For the more and more data generated by the worldwide proliferation of megabytes, the more important it will become to sift through all this noise to focus on what is really important. This requires the development of a critical faculty that too many Japanese lack, unless they have spent time abroad, for the simple reason that their education system has from an early age consciously suppressed it. This characteristic also explains why the Japanese in recent years have made such poor investors, resulting in the fiasco of their overseas property investments in the late 1980s. The ultimate trend followers, they have taken the natural human urge to run in herds to a ludicrous, almost comical, extreme. A society that fails to tolerate mavericks is a society that will miss out on the dynamics of the information revolution. For change is occurring at such a dramatic if not terrifying pace in the computer industry, in terms of the sheer rapidity of product life cycles and the intensity of downward price pressures, that a slavish devotion to a perceived conventional wisdom is a formula for repeated failure.

There is certainly no disputing that the world has embarked on a high-tech revolution every bit as profound as its industrial predecessor that began in late-eighteenth-century Britain. And America is leading the way. The revolution is based on the personal computer and it will continue to result in dramatic improvements in productivity in the workplace. The price of computers may have collapsed thanks to cutthroat competition and technological advance, but as a consequence the demand for them has soared. Edward Yardeni, chief economist at securities firm C. J. Lawrence in New York, estimates that adjusted for inflation (i.e., falling computer prices) spending on office and computer machinery rose 746 percent during the 1980s in America. Spending on high-tech equipment (a category that includes office and store machinery, communication equipment, photographic equipment and scientific and engineering instruments) accounted in 1992 for 45 percent of American companies' spending on all capital equipment, up from 18 percent fifteen years ago. Orders for communication equipment alone have doubled in the past four years.

This investment has resulted in dramatic productivity improvements as the computer industry has converged around common standards or so-called open systems, the result of the dominance of America's Microsoft in the area of software and of America's Intel in chip production. These two companies, as the dominant suppliers of microprocessors and personal computer software—the "brains" inside the personal computer and the programs that control its function—have become by far the most powerful companies in the computer industry. Yet neither company existed in the mid-1970s. This West Coast duo—Intel is based in California and Microsoft in the state of Washington—now hope to dominate the next stage of the computer revolution, which is the development of "users." That is, more powerful computers that will feed information to networks of personal computers linking them together, thereby further undermining the once dominant mainframe computer. Whether they succeed in that aim remains unclear but, in the meantime, the Japanese remain conspicuous by their absence from this mighty competitive struggle. The challenge to Intel's and Microsoft's current dominance comes from other American firms, not from the Japanese, or for that matter the Europeans.

One primary cause of the Japanese producers' problems in the computer industry lies in their long-standing failure to treat the industry as a global market. Ironically, this has its cause in the peculiarities of Japanese culture or rather language. For too long the Japanese computer industry was shielded from foreign competition because of the sheer complexities involved in designing software that could be used with the Japanese characters known as *kanji*. But that has now changed, thanks to technological advance. By 1992 American companies had entered the domestic Japanese market selling IBM-compatible personal computers equipped with kanji-friendly software that was fully bilingual. Even worse, they were undercutting the dominant Japanese producers, in terms of the prices the charged, by huge amounts. The impact has been devastating because it has exposed just how uncompetitive the Japanese, long protected in their home market, had become.

It was Compaq that made the headlines. The Texas-based producer had not rushed into Japan unprepared. It spent three years studying the Japanese market the old-fashioned way. A single employee, Tom Howard, spent this time in Japan personally developing relationships with independent distributors. This was crucial since twenty-five of the top fifty dealers in Japan are owned by the dominant producers, NEC, Fujitsu and IBM Japan. So Compaq could only sell through the remaining independent producers. The firm actually launched its product in March 1992 trying to sell its personal computer as a "quality" product (i.e., at prevailing Japanese high prices). But when this strategy did not work Compaq decided in October the same year to start discounting aggressively. In a repeat of similar tactics it had employed at home, it launched a ¥128,000 personal computer in Japan (a few months earlier it had begun a price war in America when it began selling an $890 computer), backed by an aggressive and for Japan novel marketing strategy of comparative advertising that compared the prices of its products with the dominant Japanese producers and in particular those of NEC, which had a dominant 52 percent share of the Japanese personal computer market. The theme of the campaign though was not just price cutting. Its slogan was *Jōhō-ishi*, which means literally information restoration. This was a deliberate play on the Meiji restoration of the mid-nineteenth century that belatedly launched Japan headlong into the industrial era.

The combined effect was explosive. Two thirds of Compaq's sales in 1992 occurred in the last three months of that year. But more important was the challenge its sales strategy, immediately followed by the other American makers, posed to the Japanese, whose products with their proprietary chips and software were not compatible with the IBM-Microsoft-Intel world that was suddenly available in a user-friendly way to native Japanese speakers. For the long-closed nature of the Japanese market meant that the Japanese producers were totally vulnerable if the Japanese consumer decided to opt for the open systems that now dominate outside Japan. Also because their market was only inside Japan the Japanese producers did not command the same global economies of scale enjoyed by their American competitors.

NEC is not populated by stupid people. Doubtless many within the company knew such a challenge was coming. But as a giant corporation it had become too bureaucratic and so was not able to respond convincingly to the importers' challenge. The first reaction was to launch in November a national advertising campaign explicitly attacking the Microsoft DOS/V software system. But the Japanese makers soon had to face reality and start cutting prices. By the spring of 1993 they had reduced the prices of their personal computers by about 50 percent from the levels prevailing one year before. Yet their models were still priced about 50 percent higher than equivalent American imported machines. Meanwhile, the price war had been further intensified by Dell's entry into the Japanese market in January 1993. Dell's strategy was to copy its spectacular success in the American market by selling computers over the telephone. This enabled it to reduce its prices even further by avoiding using a dealer network. Compaq responded to Dell's arrival by cutting its prices in Japan by a further 10 percent in February. The result of all this frenzied discounting is that personal computers in Japan now sell for about the same price (allowing for foreign exchange conversions) as they do in America, whereas in Europe personal computers still command a price premium over comparative American levels. The change for the Japanese consumer has been breathtaking.

The American producers have made such an effort because they realize that the personal computer market in Japan is still immature. Despite its high-tech image Japan is years behind America in the development toward data processing and paperless offices both in the private and public sectors. Walk into any office in the Ministry of Finance, the premier institution of Japan's venerated bureaucracy, and there is not a computer in sight. Desks are crammed with piles of paper as well as another rare sight in politically correct America, overflowing ashtrays. Walk into the office of a Japanese bank or trading company and hordes of similarly clad people are to be seen performing manual paper-shuffling tasks. This is the reason for Japan's appalling levels of white-collar productivity, and why there is so much for now hidden underemployment. It is precisely these ranks of white collardom that have been decimated in America as companies have embarked on seemingly continuous rounds of restructuring in recognition of the fact that the personal computer has made so many traditional office tasks redundant.

Such an employment structure cannot survive if Japan is to remain competitive, which is one major reason why the demand for personal computers will soar. There is certainly plenty of ground to make up. Some 10 million personal computers are sold every year in America compared with only 2 million at the moment in Japan. Yet in the next five years sales of personal computers in Japan should grow by at least 25 percent per annum, compared with perhaps only 15 percent in America's more mature market. America had a 43 percent share of the world personal computer market at the end of 1991. The importers will continue to have a significant price advantage over the until now dominant Japanese producers because the likes of NEC will continue to be reluctant to discount that aggressively since that would require taking dramatic cost-cutting measures, such as abandoning long-standing relationships with wholesalers and even closing dealer networks. For it is the wholly owned dealer network, with its emphasis on after-sales service, that NEC traditionally views as its major strength in the marketplace, combined of course with its proprietary operating system and large software library consisting of more than fourteen thousand titles.

It is this exclusive format that has allowed NEC to charge high prices for its software in the sure belief that it had a captive market. And it is this whole edifice that is directly threatened by the arrival in Japan of the universal DOS/V operating system. For the Japanese consumer now has a choice to stay with NEC and remain its prisoner, or to branch out and join the IBM-compatible world. NEC is naturally reluctant to abandon its own familiar world. But ominously for its future prospects in the personal computer market, all of its domestic rivals, from Fujitsu down, have now adopted DOS as the standard operating system for personal computers on grounds of pure expediency.

The long-closed nature of the Japanese computer market, the result of the complications caused by *kanji*, has also caused the Japanese to lag far behind in the key area of software. For software vendors in Japan have traditionally served only a limited domestic market and, even worse, a particular manufacturer of hardware. Because there are no common standards, most software programs have been custom-designed for a specific customer or at best groups of customers, which means they usually cannot be sold elsewhere. The result again has been an absence of economies of scale, which is one reason why Japan has no equivalent of a Microsoft or

Lotus. Instead there have traditionally been two types of software house in Japan. The first kind develops application software for mainframe computers. The second comprises those firms writing software applications for personal computers. Both sorts tended to have the same customers, since in Japan the companies that make mainframes also make personal computers. In this sense the Japanese computer companies have unthinkingly followed the disastrous IBM model since, when demand for personal computers exploded, it only served to cannibalize existing sales of mainframes. In out-of-date Japan mainframe-based programs still account for 90 percent of software sales, an extraordinary situation that will clearly change fast.

The software companies designing programs for mainframe use prospered during the Bubble primarily because they had plenty of demand for their services from the then booming financial services industry. The banks and securities companies were very eager to update their trading systems and the like. However, when the problems hit the mainframe sector, these software vendors in order to survive were forced to enter the personal computer market. This, combined with the continuing collapse in capital investment throughout the economy as a result of the domestic recession, has caused a bloodbath in Japan's software industry, which consists of many small subcontractor firms. Many of these companies were set up during the Bubble boom by youthful would-be entrepreneurs. They tended to be extremely undercapitalized and have primitive financial controls. As a result of the collapse in demand from end-users they have gone bust in huge numbers. In 1992 sixty-eight software companies failed, owing ¥10m or more (as did doubtless many more smaller firms), according to Teikoku Data Bank. By the end of September 1993 a further 105 firms had failed, owing ¥10m or more.

In the meantime, Microsoft and Lotus have embarked on a price war in the Japanese domestic market. This was a natural consequence of the price cuts that had already been announced in Japan's personal computer market. In May 1993 the two firms announced price cuts of up to 40 percent. Thus, Microsoft's Works software package on which this chapter was written, which combines a spreadsheet, word processor and data base, was reduced in price from ¥40,000 to ¥29,800. Lotus and Microsoft were competing directly with each other because there were no Japanese firms offering a competitive product, an astonishing development. Yet it is software, not hardware, that is now the profit center of the global computer industry. In other words, it is not the box itself, but what is inside it that matters. The Japanese computer giants failed totally to grasp this fundamental truth in time; to perceive that software was a product distinct and separate from hardware. Instead they have missed out on the whole dramatic transition of the computer industry. The have continued to delegate software work to subcontractors as cheaply as possible. The result has been to give the Japanese computer industry an almost dinosaur-like quality.

If they missed out on software, Japan's large computer makers have also repeated the failure of IBM precisely because they were so intent on trying to copy Big Blue. That flawed strategy consisted of remaining too committed to the mainframe computer, a business that is now threatened with demise, and grievously underestimating the impact of the personal computer. Here the biggest casualty is Fujitsu, Japan's largest computer market, whose mainframe business accounts for about thirty percent of its consolidated revenues. Fujitsu lost ¥38 billion in the year to March 1993 and it was expected to lose as much again in the first six months of the following financial year. Yet Fujitsu has yet to see the full-scale impact of the rise of the personal computer on its own business, since corporate Japan has been much slower than its American counterpart to abandon the mainframe. But as the productivity gains that have been achieved by American firms through their investment in computer networking become ever more apparent, Japanese companies will be forced also to make that transition if only to remain competitive. This again has drastic implications not only for Fujitsu's mainframe business but also for the future stability of the Japanese employment system.

This need for Japanese companies to wean themselves off mainframes and develop networks of personal computers is also the reason why America's Electronic Data Systems became in September 1993 the first foreign company to buy (for ¥2.9 billion) a Japanese software firm, the ailing Japan Systems. EDS, the Dallas-based company that successful-entrepreneur-turned failed-protectionist-populist Ross Perot founded and then sold to General Motors, doubtless hopes the acquisition will gave it greater penetration into the local corporate market, since it reckons, correctly, that its data-processing expertise will be in growing demand from Japanese companies increasingly desperate to learn the new networking techniques. Who knows, in due course EDS may even have a role to play in making Japanese government offices paperless. The American company has certainly worked for governments in other countries. As for Fujitsu, it remains very hard for it to undergo the sort of radical restructuring that has been announced in recent years by IBM. That former celebrated American guarantor of lifetime employment has already shed some 150,000 employees and more cuts are likely to follow. So far Fujitsu has only announced relatively tinkering changes. It has said it will reduce its workforce by six thousand people by 1995 via the usual voluntary retirements and transfers to group companies. And it will hire fewer graduates. This is hardly the stuff of which great corporate turnarounds are made. Greater progress seems to have been made by Toshiba. By the middle of 1993 it had embarked on a strategy of reducing by up to 40 percent its number of product lines. It has also pulled out of mainframe production. So just as with the carmakers the focus is on cost reduction and reduction of product lines.

The same familiar problems are also evident in Japan's consumer electronics industry. Just as Nissan's decision to close Zama concentrated the world's attention on the Japanese carmakers' plight, so the humiliating resignation the same week of Matsushita president Akio Tanii clearly revealed major problems in the consumer electronics industry. The move signaled the return of family control, with Yoichi Morishita becoming president under the watchful eyes of Matsushita chairman Masaharu Matsushita. Matsushita is a corporate giant with 210,000 group employees worldwide. Together with another still family-run company, namely Toyota, Matsushita symbolizes the success of exporting Japan. Both firms were famous for their cost-conscious culture, their sense of austerity and their determination to deliver quality. Yet on becoming president Morishita indicated a pending shake-up and a return to the frugal ways of old by declaring to the press that in some areas the company had become "lax and extravagant." These were terms that have never been traditionally associated with Matsushita.

It is true that the problems in the consumer electronics area are not of a similar order of magnitude to the radical structural change that faces Japan's computer makers. There is nothing akin to the sheer drama posed by the move from the mainframe to the personal computer, or the dominance of software over hardware. Still, the industry does face the deepest cyclical crunch in its history at a time when vendors appear to have run out of new product.

Japan's consumer electronics sector has been hit simultaneously by three trends. They are the global slowdown, the rise of the yen and the saturation penetration levels achieved by many major product lines in their traditionally most successful markets. The last factor is probably the hardest to overcome. After the spending binge of the 1980s consumers in the world's developed economies are simply glutted with the Japanese manufacturers' hit consumer products, nowhere more so than in gadget-mad Japan itself. A total of 99 percent of Japanese consumers had color television in March 1993, 64 percent had a video recorder, 48 percent had a CD player and 26 percent had a camcorder, according to data published by the EPA. Manufacturers have therefore had to cut prices in an attempt to keep market share and maintain operating rates at their factories. Employees were made well aware of the extent of the problems when NEC, Sanyo and other firms in the sector paid a part of their bonuses in paper vouchers that could only be exchanged for products made by their employers. This may be one way of clearing unsold inventory. But it also sent a clear "shock" message to the workforce that times were tough. Thus, section managers received vouchers for ¥100,000, department managers for ¥200,000 and senior executives for ¥300,000. This sort of retrenchment may have a symbolic impact. But it clearly is of only marginal importance financially. To really cut their costs the consumer electronics makers, like the carmakers, have already embarked on plans to reduce their number of product lines aggressively. A MITI study has concluded that in the first round of cutbacks twenty-five models of videocassette recorders and nineteen television models will be shed.

The consumer electronics firms also are moving production rapidly offshore. A survey conducted by the Tokyo office of S.G. Warburg, a British securities firm, found that overseas production accounted for 38 percent of Matsushita's and 35 percent of Sony's total production in 1993. By 1998 S.G. Warburg reckons that share will have risen to 50 percent and 45 percent respectively. The smaller firms have even more ground to make up. Sharp and Sanyo Electric had overseas production rates of 24 percent and 29 percent in 1993. S.G. Warburg reckons this will have more than doubled to 50 percent by 1998. This is all part of the familiar hollowing-out thesis. Japanese televisions, stereos, video recorders and camcorders will all increasingly be made in southeast Asia.

Such a strategy is as inevitable as it is increasingly obvious. But unlike the carmakers, the consumer electronics firms have another fundamental problem that a mere reduction in manufacturing costs will not solve. That is the lack of an obvious next hit product. Despite much optimism and even more hype this will not be high-definition television. From the Japanese point of view too much hope and again hype have also been invested in the trendy-though-vague-because-still-evolving concept of multimedia. This is the convergence of the worlds of computing, telecommunications, consumer electronics and even entertainment. This new industry may still be taking shape but the potential is clearly enormous. The trouble for the Japanese is that they are once again lagging far behind the Americans.

Consider also the tend toward "wireless" technology, which in the 1990s is likely to prove as big a boom in business terms as the personal computer was in the 1980s. Users will increasingly be liberated at an affordable price from the tyranny of land-locked telephone lines and the like. They will be able to communicate freely and increasingly cheaply. Nor will this only be communication by voice. The provision of wireless voice data will also become increasingly available as manufacturers launch a wide range of hand-held gadgets that will function as telephone, fax, notepad, computer and message center. This sort of technology will enable people literally to pull out their office files while sunning themselves on the beach or sitting on a train. Also increasingly these new machines will be able to recognize hand-written instructions as well as typed ones. Apple kicked off this whole new market when it launched its Newton "personal digital assistant" in 1993. Whether that particular product will succeed or not, and it probably will not, is besides the point. Other variations will surely follow. It was the promise of the same related boom in wireless that prompted America's AT&T to shell out $12.6 billion (and assume another $4.9 billion of debt) when it agreed to buy McCaw Cellular Communications in August 1993. This represented a huge gamble since McCaw had only 2 million cellular subscribers out of the 12 million cellular subscribers in America at the time and had never made a profit.

But it is neither ATT nor Apple that has the potential to be the biggest beneficiary of wireless. That prize actually belongs to a company whose name sounds more like it belongs in an industrial museum than at the vanguard of technological advance. The company is Motorola. Founded in 1928, this Schaumburg, Illinois, based firm is as good an example as any of the revival of American manufacturing that makes a mockery of the trendy declinism so prevalent in Washington. For Motorola dominates booming industries of our time in which the Japanese are merely marginal players. Indeed, Motorola may have the potential to be the major beneficiary of the coming boom in wireless communication. But as important, it also has claim to be America's if not the world's premier manufacturer.

Motorola is still viewed by many as primarily a microchip company. But that is only a secondary part of its business even though Motorola is second only to Intel in the production of chips and semiconductors, which accounted for 32 percent of its sales in 1992. The company is the world's dominant manufacturer of wireless equipment, a category that includes the infrastructure and handsets for cellular, paging and two-way radios in all of which Motorola is the world leader in terms of market share. This is appropriate. Motorola has been involved in wireless technology for a long time, having invented both the car radio and the walkie-talkie. The firm still defines its mission today as the pursuit of the continuing wireless revolution, which will enable growing numbers of people to speak to one another and transmit data to one another via wireless means. Sales of wireless equipment accounted for about 60 percent of total revenues of $13.3

billion last year. But if the microchips that Motorola buys from itself are included, then wireless's proportion of total sales rises to about 70 percent. It is this portion of the business that is expected to explode, with some Wall Street analysts projecting earnings growth of 25 percent per annum in the 1990s. Odd though it may sound, such a performance would give mature Motorola the profile of a hot growth company.

All aspects of wireless seem to be booming, from the well-worn to the total high-tech. Take paging, a technology that has been around for twenty years in America. Demand for pagers is soaring in developing countries because they are a cheap alternative to inefficient conventional telephone systems. Motorola has over half the world market in pagers, a share that is worth to it about $1.5 billion in annual sales. Its revenues from this product are growing by about 30 percent a year. The firm reckons, for example, that it will have shipped more than 2 million pagers to China in 1993. The only reason that India, another potentially vast market, has not yet discovered pagers is because of protracted politicking over the award of licenses. It is a similar story in cellular telephones, where Motorola has an estimated 40 percent world market share, larger than all the Japanese producers combined. Here again demand is exploding in emerging economies where cellular phone users, desperate to escape the tyranny of inefficient local monopolies, tend to generate about three times the billable minutes as do subscribers in America.

Motorola also provides the infrastructure necessary for the provision of these services. It is making lots of money building cellular networks as new consortia are formed all over the world to compete with established operators, which are often the traditional telephone companies. Anthony Langham, an analyst at NatWest Securities in New York and a self-confessed Motorola fan, reckons that between 1992 and 1994 about seventy new networks will be constructed, compared with a total of about one hundred built in the preceding thirteen years. And the more networks that are up and running, the greater will be the competition. This will mean lower prices for cellular users and so increased demand for cellular phones, which in the 1990s should shed their 1980s yuppie image as a comparative luxury item. Soaring demand in developing nations as well as in overregulated countries like Japan ($1 billion in sales) is why less than one third of Motorola's sales will be in America by 1997 as opposed to just under 50 percent in 1992.

Meanwhile, Motorola is putting its own money where its mouth is. It owns equity stakes in about forty-five wireless networks worldwide, worth perhaps $5 billion, and the firm continues to make new investments in networks as an ongoing policy. This has three benefits. Motorola builds up a portfolio of valuable assets; it usually wins the contract to build the network if it owns part of it; and it also tends to end up with a higher share of the handset business.

Motorola, to maintain its market share, must also make the right product at the right price. This depends on maintaining its so far impressive record in manufacturing, reflected in a steep increase in recent years in sales per employee. Motorola reckons it has saved more than $3 billion in the past six years by reducing defects in manufacturing. It now takes only two hours to build a cellular phone at one of its best new plants in an affluent Chicago suburb near the firm's worldwide corporate headquarters. As a company Motorola now prefers to make products near to the final customer rather than locating production in distant countries just because wages are that much lower. Motorola veteran and vice chairman John Mitchell says: "Anything that takes days or weeks to do will cost much more no matter how much lower the labor cost compared with two hours in Illinois." But such an approach requires minimal defects. Here Motorola's intelligence gatherers believe they are winning the quality game. Mitchell says the firm has "benchmarked" its competitors' manufacturing efforts, including the Japanese. "We know where everybody is and frankly we are ahead of the pack," he says. The corporate goal of this company, which is dominated at the management level by bright engineers with an entrepreneurial bent, is to reach a form of statistical nirvana known internally as "six sigma" which would mean only 3.4 defects per 1 million units produced, or in Motorola-speak, per 1 million "opportunities." Wall Street analysts used to regard sigma as just another public relations slogan when it was first introduced at the beginning of 1987. Now they are not so sure, given the dramatic improvement achieved in productivity.

Motorola has not done all this by building a bureaucracy. The firm is organized like any successful large company should be in the information age. It is highly decentralized; subdivided into numerous profit centers, each of which is headed by a product manager with responsibility for design, production and marketing. The company's philosophy is not to expand profit margins to the limit like rival chip maker Intel but rather to drive prices down by efficient production and to go for market share. Tighter profit margins are viewed as a healthy self-discipline to keep production costs low while also having the beneficial effect of keeping competitors chasing. This strategy makes sense since the penetration rates of cellular and other wireless products are so low that they are a long way from being mature markets. If Motorola were to be too greedy today, in terms of the profit margins it tries to extract, it would amount to an open invitation to competitors to try to eat away at its now dominant market shares.

Motorola also has one exciting longer-term project that could prove a bonanza. It is called Iridium. This is a satellite system that will allow users to talk to each other by cordless phone wherever they are on the planet, whereas cellular is hampered by a plethora of incompatible systems. After several years of funding all the research on Iridium, Motorola secured in August 1993 a first-round tranche of financing for this project from an international consortium now called Iridium Inc., equity in which was bought by the likes of Bell Canada, Sprint of America and various Japanese companies including Sony, Mitsubishi and Kyocera. This amounted to a considerable vote of confidence for such an ambitious venture. But perhaps as important for Motorola, Iridium Inc. has become a major new customer. Iridium Inc. signed a $3.4 billion contract for Motorola to act as primary contractor in the design and construction of the whole network, and an additional $2.8 billion contract for Motorola to maintain and operate the network for its first five years. In another spin-off, Motorola will make the subscriber equipment. Iridium, which is due to be up and running by 1998, is designed not to compete with cellular but to complement it, since it will do what other mobile phones cannot do (i.e., talk worldwide), and for that service it will doubtless charge a premium rate. But even if it proves an expensive folly, Motorola's risk is limited. Its stake in Iridium Inc. will be reduced from 34 percent to 15 percent by 1998 while in the meantime it will get the bulk of the development revenues. This seems the ideal business arrangement.

So Motorola provides a fascinating case study not only of a company that can compete effectively in the world market manufacturing in America, but also one that is about to make a lot of money in the commercial application of one of the most exciting new technologies of the continuing information revolution. And the Japanese, it should be noted, are almost invisible in this whole process. They may have missed out in computers because they lamely followed established giant IBM rather than maverick upstart Microsoft. But in wireless the Japanese are barely even players. This again is an astonishing development given the overwhelming conviction held by so many only a few years ago that the Japanese would lead the world in high-tech. Such forecasts could not have been more wrong.

In fact, the Japanese companies that are still competitive in the electronics industry are usually those that have retained an independent quality and do not play unthinkingly by conventional Japan Inc. rules. An example is Kyoto-based Kyocera, which, it is worth noting, is one of the investors in Iridium through an affiliate. Kyocera is one of the few Japanese firms that will probably see a growth in its sales and profits in 1993 at the consolidated level despite the soaring yen. Its business is based on a 65 percent share of the global $2 billion market for ceramic packaging for integrated circuits. Intel is therefore a major customer of Kyocera's. The firm is unconventional, its founder Inamouri, a self-made businessman who studied for his engineering degree in rural Kagoshima far away from elite Tokyo University. Kyocera has a cost-conscious culture that reflects these provincial origins together with a reputation for providing unstinting after-sales service to its clients. This explains the company's dominant market share in ceramic packaging, since Kyocera does not possess any particularly special proprietary technology in this area. Nor is it part of any exclusive keiretsu circle. Rather it has remained true to its origins, refraining from hiring graduates from elite universities like Tokyo and Kyoto, since such young men are probably unlikely to be sufficiently hungry. Kyocera has also shown an untypically Japanese enthusiasm for deregulation. Chairman Inamouri, who is quoted in an earlier chapter on this theme, has become particularly vocal about this cause since Kyocera's diversification into the field of telecommunications. For Inamouri, smart businessman as he is, was quicker than most to sense the opportunities offered by the wireless revolution in the heavily regulated domestic Japanese telecommunications market. But in doing so he has come right up against one of the more obdurate if not plain reactionary corners of Japan's bureaucracy.

Kyocera has a 25 percent founding stake, which is also the largest, in DDI. Established in 1984, this is the most successful of Japan's three long-distance telephone carriers. It is also an investor in Iridium. Inamouri has lobbied from the start to get DDI into the whole wireless area via mobile tele-communications, a still undeveloped area in Japan. It is an ambition that has been resisted over the years by officialdom, although DDI belatedly received a license to compete with NTT from March 1994 on in the new digital cellular market. This is the context that explains Inamouri's increasingly loud calls over recent years for deregulation. He is right to make such a lot of noise. For as the Motorola example shows, wire-less promises to be a key theme of the 1990s. Yet it is a trend that until now the stubborn Japanese bureaucracy has been actively preventing Japanese businessmen from exploiting. The result is that even if official policy now changed over-night, Japanese companies have already been put at a huge disadvantage in competing for this latest bonanza of the in-formation age. Tsuruhiko Nambu, a professor at Tokyo's Gakushuin University and chairman of a study group of ex-ecutives from NEC, Fujitsu and other firms that is lobbying officialdom to ease up on the red tape, has described the bureaucratic attitude in this vital areas as a form of "negative industrial policy."

This is no exaggeration. Multimedia may indeed prove to be one of the industries of the future. But the responsible Japanese bureaucrats do not seem to want to know. Efforts to exploit the increasingly frantic worldwide move toward an era merging voice communications with data and moving images have met in Japan a formidable obstacle. That is the Ministry of Post and Telecommunications (MPT). It represents one of the more antediluvian corners of Japan's fossilized bureau-cracy. Yet its power to mess things up remains considerable.

By unhappy coincidence two of the three key areas in multimedia fall under MPT's purview. These are broadcasting and telecommunications. Only this ministry has the authority to grant broadcasting licenses in Japan, be it ordinary radio and television, or satellite and cable TV. Likewise, the same ministry wields a heavy regulatory hand over the telecommunications industry. It also remains opposed to the broadcasting and telecommunications industries moving onto each other's turf despite the development of technology that would allow, say NTT, to send cable TV programs down an ordinary telephone line.

The practical consequences of MPT's reactionary attitudes are by now clear enough. Japan has failed so far to develop flourishing domestic industries in these areas primarily because of its heavyhanded regulation. One example is cable television. At the moment cable TV operators can only function within a limited geographical area, a political ward or *ku*. This is why the greater Tokyo area has more than twenty cable companies and why most operators lose money. Cable TV is also as a result costly. There were only 1.3 million Japanese households subscribing to cable TV in April 1993, according to the Cable Japan Advertising Bureau. True, there are signs that MPT officials have begun to realize the folly of having so many small local monopolies. Their problem now is how to reform matters without forcing many of them out of business.

Another example of Japan's backward ways is mobile telephones. MPT has consistently banned new entrants into this field. Consumers are still not able to buy mobile phones in Japan but have to rent them at a monthly cost of ¥15,000 and higher from one of three carriers. Consequently, only 1 percent of Japanese people have a mobile phone compared with 3 percent in America. Still, the potential of this market remains huge even though it for now is largely untapped, which is why shares in DDI were eagerly bought up in September 1993 when they were floated on the Tokyo stock market in the most successful initial public offering in Japan since the Tokyo bear market began in early 1990. Japan's cellular phone market has grown more than three times since the initial liberalization of the cellular market in late 1988, with the number of subscribers reaching 1.6 million in September 1992. Kleinwort Benson, the British securities firm mentioned earlier, forecasts that there will be 9 million subscribers by the year 2000. And it expects Kyocera, through its equity stake in DDI, to be the prime beneficiary among Japanese quoted companies of this growth, aside that is of course from DDI itself. This seems a quite reasonable projection of future growth, for American and European experience in recent years has been that demand for cellular services keeps growing despite recession. The basic point is that the Japanese market remains extraordinarily underdeveloped for such an affluent country.

A third example of MPT messing things up is satellite television. This has flopped in Japan, a victim of the economic slump, overoptimistic forecasts and clumsy government intervention. The biggest financial disaster has been the inappropriately named WOWOW, Japan's first commercial satellite TV service. It shows films and sundry entertainment via a broadcasting satellite. It had admitted by the beginning of 1993 to having piled up at least ¥40 billion of debts (the real financial damage was far greater) since its launch in April 1991, more than wiping out in the process its initial capital of ¥41.5 billion. This was a severe embarrassment for MPT, since the WOWOW venture was a classic example of administrative guidance gone badly wrong. For though WOWOW was owned by a private company called Japan Satellite Broadcasting (JSB), that firm in turn had no fewer than 263 corporate shareholders, all of whom had invested on the assumption that the government had effectively guaranteed their investment. For JSB was assembled by the ministry as an amalgamation of the various consortia that originally bid for Japan's first commercial satellite license. The result was an organizational nightmare since no one was in charge. WOWOW had 1.2 million subscribers by the end of 1992, well below the 3 million needed to have a hope of breaking even. The government now has to find some deft way of restructuring its debts without direct transparent use of taxpayers' money, since this would be considered politically out of the question. Satellite TV, along with designer clothes and nightclub going, is viewed in the 1990s as out-of-fashion Bubble-like conspicuous consumption.

The attitude of MPT has been so reactionary, and so contrary to Japan's economic self-interest, that it seems only a matter of time before its senior officials cave in to the mounting pressures. This will mark yet another aspect of Japan's new reality. Such a surrender will coincide with growing direct attacks on the more entrenched elements of the bureaucracy, of which MPT is one prime example, as the Finance Ministry is another. That the private sector is becoming increasingly impatient for reform is clear from the growing interest shown by MITI in this area. MITI's role in the making of Japan's post-1945 economic miracle may have been much exaggerated by Western conspiracy theorists overenamored with the powers of "Japan Inc." Still, MITI is a beacon of enlightenment compared with the folks at MPT. MITI has been prodded into action by increasingly loud complaints from the likes of NEC, Fujitsu and Toshiba, whose interests it represents. These firms are understandably frustrated. They are at the forefront of much of the technology that goes into multimedia, particularly at the component level. Yet if there is no development of domestic industries in Japan, then their role will continue to be confined to acting primarily as original equipment manufacturers (i.e., companies that build products for other companies) to sell under their own name to American and European firms.

Consequently, MITI has begun to push for some sort of

industrial policy in this area. Its problem is that it cannot push too aggressively, since only the electronics industry formally comes under its jurisdiction. Still, MITI sounded a wake-up call to MPT in January 1993 when it released a report on the role of technology in an information society. The buzz phrase was "seikatsu *jōhō-ka*". This report called for greater coordination between the two ministries in this area. There is also a MITI-sponsored lobbying group, a so-called information network study group, whose membership includes the big electronics firms, broadcasters and telecommunications firms. Eventually MPT will succumb to these pressures if only because younger officials will rise to the top of the ministry who are more aware of modern technological possibilities. The real question is how long this will take to happen and how far by then Japan will have been left behind as a result of the actions of its increasingly obsolete bureaucratic structure, a bureaucracy that has continued to remain myopically focused on more familiarly conventional obsessions such as Japan's trade surplus with America and the rest of the world.

7

Foreign Policy and Trade— End of an Era

CALL IT the feel-good summit. Political theater was the chief feature of the G7 Summit held in Tokyo in July 1993, the annual jamboree for leaders of the world's rich nations. Spice was added to the occasion by the fact that Japan was in the middle of a surprise general election campaign. Still it was American president Bill Clinton who set the tone of the proceedings on his first overseas trip as president. Amidst his usual blathering on about "change," Clinton found time to press the flesh in a stroll through a crowded Tokyo shopping area, preside over a question-and-answer session at Waseda, one of Tokyo's top private universities, and telephone the surprised parents of a Japanese student who had been shot to death in Louisana a few months earlier when he had knocked on the front door of a garishly decorated house of a paranoid gun holder, believing it was the address of a Halloween party he was to attend. All this played well in Japan. Clinton's comparative youth and populist methods made a stark contrast to the seeming remoteness of many of Japan's aging politicians.

Yet the summit also brought some apparent "hard" news for the thousands of foreign journalists who had descended on Tokyo for the annual media circus. That took the form of an apparent agreed deal on the long-stalled General Agreement on Tariffs and Trade GATT negotiations on international trade as well as a bilateral agreement between America and Japan also on the vexed trade issue. Both developments were unexpected. So both caused at least temporary relief. For the initial rhetoric of members of the Clinton administration had threatened a breakdown in relations with Japan in what is often rightly described as the most important bilateral relationship in the world. Still, the relief will prove short-lived since the agreements reached at the Tokyo summit have glossed over too many difficult issues, the result of both Clinton's and perhaps more importantly then outgoing Japanese prime minister Kiichi Miyazawa's desire for a deal. For the issues raised by the American side since Clinton's inauguration indicate that America has begun to question the very fundamentals of Japan's post-1945 political order and its relations with the United States. The nation that set in motion the successful rebuilding of Japan after the Second World War has begun to wonder about the benefits of the system it produced.

The new American way of thinking has been clearly articulated by administration officials. Take Mickey Kantor, the belligerent U.S. trade representative in the Clinton administration. In a speech to the House of Representatives Budget Committee in April 1993, he said with regard to the issue of Japan's trade surplus: "We expect to hold Japan to its past promises and agreements . . . and believe that quantifiable results are necessary." As Morgan Stanley's Tokyo-based investment strategist, Alexander Kinmont, observed at the time: "The early part of the sentence could have been uttered at any point over the past ten years. However, the second part is new.* Not only was it new but it threatened the very

* *"Japan: Trade and Politics,"* Morgan Stanley Investment Perspectives, *April 26, 1993.*

foundation of the American-Japanese alliance, which has endured so effectively since the end of the American Occupation in 1951. That postwar settlement was based on Japan being accorded extraordinarily generous access to export to America's giant consumer market in return for both a pacifist Japan remaining solidly pro-American and anti-communist in the then strategically critical Northeast Asian region and agreeing to American troops to be stationed on its soil. In other words, Japan voluntarily subordinated itself to the status of a comparative political and military eunuch, with no effective ability to launch foreign policy initiatives on its own, in return for unhindered access to the American market. This was the essence of the deal agreed by Japan's first important postwar prime minister, Shigeru Yoshida, at the 1951 San Francisco Peace Conference. Miyazawa, a former Finance Ministry bureaucrat, was Yoshida's secretary at that peace conference and in terms of his political philosophy has remained strongly committed ever since to this postwar settlement and opposed to those more nationalistic voices within the LDP who have long argued that the 1951 constitution humiliatingly reduced Japan's national status to that of a mere American dominion.

The rhetoric employed by Kantor and others therefore threatens the very basis of Japan's pacifist constitution and indeed its political status quo. For it has made brutally clear what should already have become apparent to Japan's political and diplomatic establishment. That is that with the end of the Cold War America can now be expected to put its commercial and economic self-interest ahead of strategic considerations. In terms of Washington power politics this means that the State Department will no longer have the last word over the Commerce Department in the making of Japan policy. It is already clear that the debate about Japan within the Clinton administration begins from an entirely different starting point than was the case with the preceding Republican administrations, which, despite the perennial trade disputes, were about as pro-Tokyo as anyone in the Japanese government could reasonably hope for given both the level and the persistence of the trade surplus.

An important point here, already previously noted, is the strong influence within the Clinton administration of the so-called revisionist school of thought. This requires some elaboration. Revisionists argue that Japan operates a different sort of capitalism than the West, designed to benefit the producer rather than the consumer, and that therefore the normal rules of free trade do not apply. Consequently, managed-trade solutions are not only appropriate but also the only effective way of dealing with the country's huge trade surplus because Japan plays by a different set of rules. Now, it is true there are many aspects of Japan that appear different, be they practices in the workplace, social customs or the education system. But that is not to say that the country is not vulnerable to market forces as the revisionists used to contend before the bursting of the Bubble demolished their case. In truth, Japan is far more like the West than many Japanese experts, with their huge vested professional interest in making the place seem more weird and different than it really is, are usually prepared to acknowledge. The Japanese consumer, to cite just one example, is as interested in a bargain as any other consumer. However, the revisionist school also struck a chord with liberal (in the American sense of the word) intellectuals in the Clinton administration not only because they were naturally attracted to isms that contended that free market capitalism could be beaten but also because it complemented the then fashionable declinist school of thought popularized by a group of American academics including Clinton's labor secretary, Robert Reich. Indeed there was a direct link between these two schools of thought or isms. Author Ian Buruma has noted that when discussing the subject of America's decline, revisionists "tend to sound like French nationalists after losing the war with Prussia in 1871. It is as though the virility of the nation was at stake."* Thus the declinists are fond of arguing, oddly, that American industry suffers from declining productivity and competitiveness. And usually their favorite point of comparison is Japan. Since such declinists tend to have anti-capitalist sympathies it has suited their purposes to argue that Japan has succeeded by avoiding free market methods. In fact of course the truth is rather more complicated than these academics in their ivory towers imagine. In recent years much of American industry has made itself ruthlessly efficient, in particular by slashing surplus jobs in the white-collar area and by investing in technology. As a result, productivity has risen. By contrast, Japanese industry's continued adherence to the post-1945 lifetime employment system, and the consequent loss of management flexibility in cutting costs, has caused corporate Japan to suffer a real loss of competitiveness vis-à-vis its American competition, especially when combined with the convergence in the cost of capital. The danger, if there is one, is actually not that American industry is declining but rather that the new costs the Clinton administration seeks to impose on the economy, in the form of high taxes and health care reform, will cause a reversal of American business's renaissance; a revival which has much to do with its companies' leading edge in the key field of information technology.

If the revisionists and their declinist friends are hopelessly behind the tide of events in the commercial marketplace, their ideas do reflect recent intellectual fashion. Consequently, they are politically influential in Washington, which makes them important. By contrast, the free traders are to a degree on the run. Even those members of the Clinton administration associated with a pro–free trade position feel obliged to single out Japan as a special case where the normal rules do not apply. An example is Lawrence Summers, a former Harvard economics professor and now undersecretary

* New York Review of Books, *March 25, 1993.*

for international affairs at the U.S. Treasury Department. In a speech to the Japan Society in New York in 1993 Summers could not have made his position more clear. He stated that economics was "central" to America's relationship with Japan and that Japan's "selective engagement" (note the phrase) in the world economy, as shown in the low level of important penetration in its economy, had persisted despite the liberalization of most formal border restrictions and traditional nontariff barriers. As a result, Summers said that America was developing a new framework for addressing these problems that would focus "less on process and more on results."

The traditional free trade argument against this sort of position is clear. Bilateral trade deficits with particular countries are ultimately mere bookkeeping items of no economic significance. What matters is that Japan recycles its overall trade surplus with the world in a constructive manner that promotes global economic activity. For ultimately the consumer can only benefit from the free flow of trade between borders. No protectionist arguments, however pseudosophisticated in construction, can overcome this undeniable fact.

The problem is of course that economics is not the only issue here. The political reality is that by 1993 Japan's trade surplus, bilateral and multilateral, remained stubbornly high. This was fast becoming politically intolerable to the country's major trading partners. The trade surplus reached 120 billion in 1993, up from $105 billion in 1992. The politically sensitive bilateral trade surplus with America reached $51 billion, an increase on 1992's $44 billion figure. Japan, it should be noted, also has a significant trade surplus with Europe and a fast-rising surplus with the rest of Asia. The result is that the country is all but friendless on the trade issue and extremely exposed to a full-scale protectionist backlash. Indeed, the wonder is that there has not been more aggressive protectionism already, given the unemployment rates in some countries, especially in Europe. But that there has not been such a reaction so far is certainly no guarantee that it will never happen since the political pressures are immense.

There is also another more compelling argument for tougher action. In the 1990s Japan has ceased to recycle its trade surplus in a way that benefits the global economy. During the 1980s much of that surplus was spent on building factories overseas or buying foreign securities, such as American Treasury bonds. So Japanese investment generated jobs or Japanese money helped finance America's or other countries' budget deficits. During the 1990s, however, a large part of the surplus has been spent repaying debt taken on in the 1980s or bolstering up problematic balance sheets at home in Japan. Japanese banks, for example, have spent billions of dollars repaying short-term Eurodollar debt they had incurred funding their mostly insane international lending activities during the 1980s to finance hotel construction and the like in places like Hawaii and Australia's Gold Coast. The Japanese banks financed this lending spree by borrowing short to lend long. By June 1990 the Japanese banks had borrowed some ¥186 trillion offshore, about ¥69 trillion of which had been subsequently lent out. These were the borrowings that were now being paid off, especially where the money subsequently lent out could be easily recovered. This was not always the case. Clearly if short-term Eurodollar debt had been taken on to finance a loan to a Los Angeles office tower or a leveraged buyout or some other such 1980s deal, as it often was, not all the principal lent would be recoverable.

The way the surplus has been recycled also helps to explain the yen's sharp appreciation in the first half of 1993. A fast-growing economy is meant to boost a currency's value. But the opposite has lately been the case for Japan. The weaker the domestic economy the greater has been the strength of the yen as Japanese entities have repatriated yen to shore up sagging balance sheets at home or to purchase yen-denominated securities having sold foreign currency-denominated ones. Such strategies clearly did little to bolster economic activity abroad, or for that matter at home, since the rising yen merely added to the downward pressure on exporters' shrunken profit margins. Instead, to quote one Japanese investment banker, Japan has become "the big black hole" of the world economy. This is not a characteristic that is likely to win friends in trade negotiations.

Japan is therefore vulnerable not only to the usual charge of exporting its way out of recession but also of exporting its post-Bubble domestic distress. A wholesale liquidation of Japanese-owned properties abroad, a process that has now begun, would make this crystal clear. In this context the usual American demands for Japan to boost its domestic consumption by deregulating its economy to produce what Summers would doubtless describe as a constructive engagement with the world economy can only be expected to grow. If Japan continues to resist or even simply to ignore such demands, even if only out of sheer political paralysis rather than stubborn opposition, confrontation seems certain. For it does not require much historical vision to understand that consistently to run such large surpluses with the rest of the industrialized world at a time of near stagnant economic activity in the G7 countries is politically out of the question. The snag is that Japan's political leaders and their bureaucratic masters tend to lack just that sort of historical understanding, which is why it will probably require a tremendous cathartic shock to force them to change policy. That could either be a protectionist shock or, more likely, the belated realization that only domestic deregulation and the resulting boost to consumption can provide the renewed level of economic growth they seek at home. One point is sure. To adopt such a pro-consumption strategy will require on the part of the political, bureaucratic and business elite a conscious admission that the post-1945 system based on heavy capital spending and pursuit of market share in export markets no longer works. That admission is not so far off since it has already begun to be recognized in the business and political community. The bureaucracy will be the last to own up to Japan's new reality. Meanwhile, what is apparent is that the Clinton administration has already made it very clear that the old arrangement is due for renegotiation.

The more activist approach the Americans will increasingly be prepared to take can be illustrated with one example. Lurking in Japan's ¥13.2 trillion supplementary budget unveiled in April 1993 was an intriguing proposal. As part of a plan to create a "new social infrastructure," the Japanese government said it would buy 330,000 personal computers between 1993 and 1996 for use in state schools. The grand vision that ultimately lies behind this so-called new infrastructure is a computerized Japan packed with fiber-optic information "highways."

Leading the lobbying effort for such an initiative in the school system was Tadahiro Sekimoto, chairman of NEC, Japan's largest seller of personal computers. The proposal, however, caught the attention of America's trade negotiators, who feared that the estimated ¥200 billion school project would amount to little more than a taxpayer-funded bailout of Japan's struggling computer makers—such as NEC, which made its first ever consolidated loss, of ¥44 billion, in the financial year that ended in March 1993. Personal computers are NEC's most profitable product. With a 52 percent share of the domestic market, the company dominates Japan's personal computer industry. However, this dominance, as already noted, is threatened, as a result of both domestic recession and foreign competition. Total sales of personal computers in Japan fell by 8 percent in the fiscal year that ended in March 1993. Battered by competing models selling for less than half the price of their own machines from the likes of Apple, Compaq and Dell, NEC belatedly announced big price cuts in February 1993. But even after this move, its computers still sold for about ¥150,000 more than those of its

foreign rivals. Naturally Japanese consumers noticed the difference. Hence the desire for Japanese government help in clearing warehouses of all those unwanted Japanese personal computers. There was certainly a national need. The average Japanese secondary school has thirteen computers; the average elementary school only four. NEC has had until now a tight grip on the school market, though there is no universal standard. Its nearest competitor is Fujitsu. Foreign firms are not a force. Apple has been successful selling to schools in other countries but has so far failed to make an impact in Japan (apart from selling to private schools).

American trade negotiators wanted to change that. Their view was that there is nothing wrong with government schemes to spend money on personal computers so long as foreign firms have a fair chance to bid for orders. This seemed doubtful in view of Japanese officials' announcements that the supplementary budget was designed to boost only domestic firms. Nonetheless, any sign that the Japanese government is buying exclusively from domestic personal computer manufacturers will be seen by the Americans as confirmation of its intention to bail out NEC and others with disguised subsidies. In an industry where Americans argue (correctly) that they are more competitive on both product and price, that would be undoubtedly provocative. Computers and computer components are America's second biggest manufactured export to Japan, after airplanes. Moreover, America's computer industry is just the sort of high-skill, high-wage industry Clinton has said he wants to promote. Certainly, for the American government to lobby to sell products for which Japanese consumers are voting with their wallets will make a refreshing change from lobbying for lemons from Detroit as George Bush found himself doing so futilely on his ill-fated trip to Tokyo at the beginning of 1992.

If the Clinton administration has changed the terms of the trade debate, the Japanese response to the increasingly

aggressive rhetoric from Washington about the need for results in trade policy was also more vigorous than usual. Traditionally when Japan has faced pressure from abroad, especially from big brother America, it would either give in reluctantly or keep quiet and hope the fuss would go away. However, on this occasion it was felt in Tokyo that the open demands for a "results-oriented" trade policy and the proposed formal setting of import targets could neither be ignored nor conceded to, since that would amount to a formal acceptance of a departure into a new regime of managed trade. Consequently, Japan decided to stage a frank attack on managed trade and at the same time to undertake a detailed defense of its own record on trade. This was contained in the Ministry of International Trade and Industry's annual white paper on trade, which was published in the summer of 1993. The white paper on this occasion did not just consist of the bureaucrats' customary dry analysis of the data. It also sought to put Japan's side of the argument in an area of policy that has usually been dominated by American and European critiques. Besides making worthy pro–free trade noises, such as the need for a multilateral GATT-style approach to trade rather than a bilateral one, the MITI report argued that Japan was in fact more open than most other countries. It noted that Japan's average tariff on mining and manufactured goods was 2.7 percent, compared with a 4.2 percent in America and 4.6 percent in the European Community. The report rejected head on the argument that Japan requires special trade sanctions because it operates a different sort of capitalism. It also sought to analyze the various components that make up the trade surplus. One defense MITI made is that most trade statistics ignore services. MITI estimated, using data from the Bank of Japan, that if Japan's imports of services had been included in its trade statistics, then the country's trade surplus would only be about $80 billion in 1992, which would have been nearly $50 billion lower than the figure actually

reported. Exclusive attention to trade in goods, the normal focus of newspaper headline writers, can therefore be misleading. Consequently, the white paper called for better collection of statistics for trade in services by international bodies such as the Organization for Economic Cooperation and Development.

The MITI report also sought to provide a theoretical justification for the continued rise in Japan's trade surplus. It went as follows: because of the recession at home Japan has suffered a steep decline in expensive imports of luxuries, which were enormously fashionable during the second half of the 1980s. This effect has been compounded, thanks to slow growth elsewhere, by low prices for the international commodities that Japanese industry depends upon. Hence, imports have collapsed. Exports of Japanese machinery, on the other hand, have withstood the downturn quite well because the Asian economies that buy them have continued to enjoy relatively robust growth. Also, the American and Japanese economies have been out of kilter. America's strengthening economy has caused an increase in American demand for Japanese imports, while Japanese demand for foreign goods had declined. The effect was amplified, MITI argued, because 35 percent of American exports to Japan are industrial commodities that are highly sensitive to the business cycle.

Having argued that criticism of the trade surplus in Washington was misconceived, the MITI white paper went on to predict that the surplus would, of its own accord, gradually diminish in size and relevance for the following reasons. First, when Japanese demand picks up again, imports will grow more quickly than in past recoveries. This is because the volume of Japanese imports has become more sensitive to the domestic economic cycle. Second, parts and components account for a growing share of Japan's exports; 28 percent of total exports and 36 percent of machinery exports in 1992 compared with 19 percent and 28 percent respectively in

1981. MITI believes that such exports should be of less concern to advocates of managed trade than consumer goods because components increase the competitiveness (and therefore the export potential) of the industries that buy them. Third, the white paper argued that from now on Japan's overseas plants will increasingly export their output back to Japan, whereas previously they bought Japanese exports of equipment and parts. Fourth and finally, the white paper subscribed to the view that the philosophy of Japanese business was changing. Having already suffered three years of declining profits following their overinvestment of the late 1980s and with every prospect of facing a fourth year of declining earnings, Japanese managers would henceforth act more like Western managers putting profits before considerations of market share. So, if in the past Japanese firms have been export-driven, in the future they will be less likely to try to export their way out of trouble.

For the above reasons, the white paper argued, hopefully but not unreasonably, Japan's trade surplus would fall in due course. However, it added that a persistent surplus (albeit a smaller one) was inevitable as long as Japanese households saved more than American ones, and America's budget deficit remained untamed. These are familiar points. But what was new was the coherent, almost transparent, way in which Japan laid out its own case. Many foreign critics naturally disputed the arguments made; some even dismissed them as pure propaganda, arguing that what was at issue was less the overall balance of trade than the issue of access to Japan's markets. Still, that MITI chose to adopt such a form of advocacy at all was a significant departure from the usual do-nothing-and-wait-for-*gaiatsu* approach that both American and European trade negotiators have found so exasperating in the past.

When the world's rich nations actually met in Tokyo for the G7 Summit, the trade dispute did not boil over into open conflict as the presummit rhetoric had suggested it might. In fact, forms of deals were actually announced. This was not because of a renewed faith in free trade per se. Rather it marked a response to certain short-term political pressures. The ever flexible Clinton, with his popularity at the time plummeting, was in the midst of a swing to the political right and was sensitive to strident press criticism that he was supporting crude protectionism. A Republican veteran of the Reagan White House, David Gergen, had been hired as communications director a few weeks prior to the summit, and following his appointment the line on trade softened significantly, both rhetorically and for that particular political moment substantively. Gergen is less a man of ideas and policies than the consummate Washington media spin doctor. As for Miyazawa, with a general election facing him as a result of his defeat over political reform in a no-confidence vote in the lower house of the Diet, he was anxious personally to have something concrete agreed at the Tokyo summit to prove to posterity he was not a total lame duck.

International press attention in Tokyo focused on the so-called Quad agreement among America, the European Community, Japan and Canada. This amounted to a draft tariff-cutting deal with the proposed elimination of tariff and nontariff barriers for eight categories of manufactured products. While the details would still have to be confirmed in subsequent negotiations and while the most contentious areas such as agriculture and financial services were left out of the agreement, this overhyped "market access package" did at least show a renewed political commitment to keep GATT going. However, that the agreement was nowhere near as big a deal as the press headlines suggested was clear from the response of the world's financial markets, which failed completely to respond to the news.

If the international press concentrated on the Quad agreement, the bilateral discussions between Japan and

America were arguably more important since trade in the post–Cold War era seems likely to be the issue that will determine this key diplomatic relationship. Here again the discussions immediately before and after the summit produced more than the complete lack of progress that was expected prior to the Tokyo gathering. Still, the deal such as it is may have raised expectations on the American side that will prove impossible for the Japanese to fulfill. That could subsequently provoke an ever worse reaction from Washington. It is certainly far too premature to write off the prospect of trade wars.

The Americans came to Tokyo with some quite specific proposals. The aim was to agree to a bilateral "framework" in which the two sides could discuss the trade issue. The American demands included the following macroeconomic targets: a cut in Japan's current account surplus to under 2 percent of its gross domestic product from the current level of over 3 percent, and a one third rise in Japan's imports of manufactured products to 4 percent of its GDP. The Americans also wanted to set market access targets in the following areas: government procurement, follow-up of past trade agreements, deregulation in financial services and other industries, and the level of direct foreign investment in Japan. Until the eve of the summit the Japanese side continued publicly to resist all such targets as managed trade and contrary to the spirit of the free trade system. However, at the eleventh hour the then outgoing prime minister Miyazawa came up with a compromise counterproposal for "reference indicators." The point of these seemed to be that Japan would accept that certain statistical measures could be monitored, provided America would agree it would take no punitive bilateral action against Japan if it failed to meet such targets. Quite what was meant by this woolly phrase was left deliberately unclear, though even this concession threatened to undermine the Japanese government's hitherto strong stance against any form of targets. Certainly, that seemed to be the fear of powerful sections of the bureaucracy who feared a deal may have been done over their heads. That was the message of an article published in the *Yomiuri Shimbun*, the daily newspaper, in the middle of the Tokyo summit that quoted anonymously as senior MITI official as saying that Miyazawa's counterproposal of reference indicators "would only serve as a reference by which we will compare the past and present and review the results." He added that, "It will not be a pledge that will continue into the future."

These comments reflected MITI's as well as the Finance Ministry's opposition even to reference indicators, though the far less powerful Ministry of Foreign Affairs was in favor of them in the interest of appeasing America. Still, a deal was agreed by an eager Miyazawa immediately after the conclusion of the summit over a sushi dinner with Clinton at Tokyo's Okura Hotel, where the American delegation was staying. Interestingly, the point man in the discussions on the Japanese side was Hisashi Owada, father-in-law to the heir to the imperial throne and also a senior Foreign Ministry official. However, Miyazawa and the Foreign Ministry may live to regret their enthusiasm. Within days it was clear from press reports and from discussions with those involved that both sides had rather different views of what the bilateral deal actually meant. Immediately following the agreement, American officials spoke of an informal understanding having been reached that the trade surplus should be reduced to 2 percent of the GNP. However, Japan's chief trade negotiator, Sozaburo Okamatsu, who was also vice minister for international affairs for MITI, said on July 14 in a lunch with the foreign press only five days after the bilateral framework agreement was announced that there was no specific number in the agreement on how much Japan should reduce its trade surplus as a percentage of the GNP. But he added that Japan had agreed in the framework agreement to pursue a "highly significant decrease" in its trade surplus over the medium term. The issue therefore becomes the somewhat semantic one of what is meant by "highly significant." Okamatsu also was conveniently vague on what was meant by "medium term," though when pressed by reporters' questioning he mentioned a period of five years. The Finance Ministry also has let its displeasure with the framework agreement be known. A senior official was quoted in the press as saying, pointedly, that the accord did not oblige Japan to stimulate its economy in order to help reduce its trade surplus.

With these sorts of noises coming out of the bureaucracy it seems clear that Miyazawa had gone over the heads of Japan's most powerful ministries, backed only by the comparative amateurs at the Foreign Ministry, who in the hierarchy of the Japanese bureaucracy come well down the totem pole. These professional diplomats also had a poor track record. In recent years the Foreign Ministry has made an unfortunate habit of raising expectations about Japan's foreign policy commitments that it has subsequently not been able to deliver on. A good example was over Japan's contribution to the Allied effort in the Gulf War where Japan was severely criticized for its reluctance to become involved after the Foreign Ministry initially had encouraged unrealistic hopes of a greater quasi-military commitment. Finally, Japan ended up with the worst of both worlds. It paid a total contribution of $13 billion toward the war effort, a substantial amount, for which it received barely a thank-you. If the Foreign Ministry has again overreached, in terms of a bilateral trade deal with America that has not got the requisite bureaucratic support within Japan, the subsequent deterioration in bilateral relations will be that much worse because the ever self-righteous Americans will sense that Japan has reneged on yet another agreement.

The politics of trade are one matter. But it is unfortunate that the Clinton administration, influenced as it is with the trendy nostrums of revisionism and declinism, has become so obsessed ideologically with economic targets, be they macro or sectoral in nature. For the Japanese are right in deriding this sort of policy orientation as a crudely protectionist form of managed trade. It is also unnecessary because America's increasingly competitive companies do not need that sort of help. Indeed, the irony is that corporate Japan is probably far better suited to prosper in a managed-trade cartelized environment than are American firms. A far better approach for the American side to adopt only gets a subordinate mention in the framework agreement though it is the area of policy that all Japan's trade partners, and not just the United States, should focus on to a far greater extent than they have done to date. This issue is the lack of foreign direct investment in Japan.

There is a well-known saying in Japan that the nail which sticks out gets hammered down. But when it comes to foreign direct investment, it is Japan that is sticking out and to an embarrassing extent. Foreign direct investment—or rather the lack of it in Japan—is worthy of greater attention. It was the theme of a study published in early 1993 by the Wednesday Group, a Washington-based congressional policy caucus made up of leading Republican members of Congress.* The study sought to counter the arguments of the managed traders who were then making the running in Washington and who were calling for increasingly aggressive retaliation against Japan for its purportedly closed market. The Wednesday Group's theme is that trade and investment are intimately linked; and that the gross imbalance in direct investment is the biggest reason for Japan's persistent trade surplus. The group argues that overseas subsidiaries of American companies in Japan import vastly more from their factories and suppliers in the United States than they export from Japan, especially when they are majority-controlled by the American

* *"Beyond Revisionism: Toward a New U.S.-Japan Policy for the Post Cold War Era,"* March 1993.

parent. As a result, direct investment stimulates imports into the country where the investment takes place.

The Wednesday Group study was partly influenced by a book published in 1992 by Dennis Encarnation, a Harvard Business School professor.* His thesis again is that the gross imbalance in direct investment is the major reason for Japan's stubbornly persistent trade surplus. Encarnation argues persuasively that inward investment is not an alternative to imports, as many protectionists once argued, but actually encourages them. This is especially true in the case of America and Japan. Encarnation's calculations showed that sales in America by local, Japanese-owned factories, assembly plants and warehouses are twice the value of all Japanese exports to America. One consequence of this is that the decline of the American dollar against the yen since 1985 has done little to improve the bilateral trade balance. Such devaluations have had limited influence on intracompany shipments between Japanese parent companies and their overseas subsidiaries because firms are reluctant to drop their own subsidiaries as suppliers in favor of a domestic rival unless the devaluation is huge and seemingly sustained. Encarnation's book also stresses the differences in the investment strategies of American and Japanese multinationals in each other's countries. Both groups of firms prefer to have majority control of overseas affiliates. But the Japanese have stuck almost exclusively to this formula in America. However, most American firms have only a minority stake in their Japanese units, a legacy of Japanese controls on inward investment that were abolished only in 1980. By then costs of yen-denominated assets had soared, making it that much more difficult and expensive to obtain a majority stake in a Japanese firm, a point that will be pursued later.

This different pattern of ownership matters because

* Rivals Beyond Trade: America Versus Japan in Global Competition (Ithica, N.Y.: Cornell University Press, 1992).

majority-controlled overseas subsidiaries import far more from their parent at home than do those subsidiaries in which the parent has only a minority stake. For only with majority ownership do multinational companies wield sufficient managerial clout to decide whether subsidiaries import supplies from their parents. As a practical matter a manager in Honda's Ohio car plant is unlikely to have the power to buy parts locally without checking with the Tokyo head office first. But a manager at Mazda (in which Ford has a 24 percent stake) back in Japan would probably not think twice about buying parts locally before calling Detroit. Encarnation argues tellingly that this is a key factor in the bilateral trade between Japan and America because the scale of "intracompany" trade between the two countries is high and dominated by Japanese firms both ways. He calculates that more than two thirds of all American imports from Japan are shipped "intracompany" (from Nissan, say, to its American subsidiaries). By contrast, intracompany trade contributed barely 50 percent of all American exports to Japan, and the majority of such shipments in this direction, ironically, were by Japanese subsidiaries to their parents back home. In fact, Japanese-owned subsidiaries in America are by far the largest American-based exporters to Japan. This, according to Encarnation, "guarantees Japanese multinationals uncontested control over bilateral trade." True, such intracompany trade also forms a big part of America's trade with other industrial countries. Encarnation's calculation shows it accounts for more than two fifths of total American imports and more than one third of total American exports. However, America's direct investment in Japan is tiny compared with its investments in Europe and other major export markets. Consequently, its ability to export to Japan is severely limited.

This raises the critical issue of why there is so little foreign direct investment in Japan and what to do about it. The lack of such direct investment is certainly glaring. Although it has the world's second largest economy, Japan has the lowest level of foreign direct investment per person of all the industrial countries: $180, compared with $1,600 in Germany, some $2,000 in America and more than $4,000 in Britain, according to data compiled by the Wednesday Group. Japan's stock of foreign direct investment totaled $22.8 billion in March 1992, with less than half coming from America. Meanwhile, Japan's total direct overseas investment amounted to $252 billion. Thus, Japan has more than twenty times more money invested abroad than is invested by other countries in Japan. Naturally, there are many arguments to explain why such a vast discrepancy exists. They include foreigners' lack of long-term commitment, informal barriers to entry posed by Japan's *keiretsu* families of firms, cultural differences and even rank discrimination by government agencies. However, the Wednesday Group's study suggests persuasively that the real issue is what should motivate any rational businessman. That is cost, and in particular in more recent years the sky-high cost of Japanese land and financial assets. The congressional group cites a 1990 survey of 340 American companies conducted for the American Chamber of Commerce in Japan. Some 55 percent of respondents said that the "high cost of doing business" was the chief deterrent to investing in Japan. By contrast, only 22 percent cited nontariff barriers and 31 percent Japanese government regulations. Overall, 64 percent of companies gave the cost of land as the main factor constraining their ability to expand in Japan. The Wednesday Group also did its own survey, quizzing 284 of the largest American firms operating in Japan. The companies' responses suggest that they do not consider the cards to be unfairly stacked against them. Only 3 percent said that the Japanese market was closed, whereas 70 percent described the market as open provided a long-term commitment was made. Again, the chief constraint preventing that sort of commitment was the sheer cost of acquiring physical assets such as factories, warehouses and land itself.

The good news is that in recent years Japanese land prices have fallen sharply, as indeed has the acquisition price of Japanese companies listed on the stock market. This in theory should do more to boost investment in Japan by foreign firms, be it by purchasing physical facilities or by buying companies through the stock market, than any amount of government deregulation. But so far asset deflation in Japan, via the stock market and property market crash, has not trigged more active corporate restructuring through foreign acquisition. One major reason why not is that the Japanese government has gone out of its way to prevent the two major asset markets, property and shares, from clearing. The risk is therefore that a great opportunity will be forfeited to close the direct investment gap and thereby increase Japan's true engagement in the world economy through more foreign direct investment in the country. America's trade negotiators should therefore focus their attacks far more on the Japanese government's crudely interventionist efforts to support its stock market and to freeze artificially its property market rather than trying to force Japanese consumers to buy specific amounts of American goods, which at the end of the day is what the pursuit of "results" in trade amounts to. Such an approach would also highlight the inconsistency between MITI's stance as expressed in the white paper that Japan believes in free trade in goods and services (as opposed to managed trade) and the Finance Ministry's overt use of administrative guidance to intervene in the stock market and so many other areas; interventions that are totally contrary to the spirit of what is usually meant by free trade.

Japan's conspicuous lack of foreign direct investment becomes all the more controversial when the country's recent history is considered. For during the early twentieth century many American firms established large market shares in Japan's domestic market. Indeed, the first three decades of this century were anomalous in Japanese history in that they marked a rare if not unprecedented period when there were no severe restrictions on foreign investment in Japan. However, the rise of militarism in the 1930s put an end to that. American companies were forced greatly to reduce their operations or even shut them down. This is why it is perhaps rather unfair to attack these same companies for refusing to make a long-term commitment to the country, given both the increasing costs involved and the history, since in many cases they had been effectively ordered out of the country once before.

That this indeed was many companies' experience is clear from a history of American multinationals in Japan by Mark Mason, a professor at Yale University.* Total stock of American direct investment in Japan, which stood at some $61.4 million in 1930, had declined to just $37.7 million ten years later as a result of the increasingly hostile environment. Take the case of the carmakers. Ford and General Motors controlled more than 95 percent of the domestic Japanese car market by 1930. The Japanese government had not blocked their entry into the market. Indeed, the city of Osaka did everything it could to encourage both Ford and GM to set up production in its area, just as American states competed vigorously to attract Japanese car plants in the 1980s by offering a range of incentives.

Ford was sufficiently committed to buy a nine-acre site near Yokohama where it built a factory in 1929. The investment was considered justified because the company's Japanese operations were so profitable. Mason relates how Ford's main competitor, GM, earned on average more than an an-

* American Multinationals and Japan: The Political Economy of Japanese Capital Control, 1899–1980 (*Cambridge, Mass.: Harvard University Press, 1992*).

nual 25 percent on its equity investment in Japan between 1927 and 1931. Yet by 1940 the Japanese operations of both Ford and GM had been reduced to "little more than a shell," to quote Mason.

The Japanese government's actions against the American producers began with a steep rise in the tariff rate for imported car parts to 40 percent. At the same time pressure began to be exerted to persuade the American subsidiaries to sell part of their Japanese operations to local interests. Interestingly, GM and Ford chose to react to the growing nationalistic pressures in different ways. GM decided to look for a local partner based on the view that it was better to own half of something real than 100 percent of almost nothing. Consequently in 1933 GM agreed to a cross-ownership arrangement with Nissan, though in order to get the military's approval, GM was told it would have to transfer 51 percent ownership to Nissan's fledgling auto subsidiary rather than only the 49 percent it wanted to sell. Finally with military pressure growing all the time and with the Nissan side demanding more and more, GM agreed in 1935 to a merger whereby Nissan would completely absorb GM Japan in exchange for GM owning 49 percent of the Japanese carmaker as well as some form of cash payment. Yet by early 1936 the climate had become so hostile that GM decided to end all merger talks with Nissan.

If GM did try to find a local partner Ford opted for a strategy of defiant independence whereby it sought to cement its presence in the market by establishing a fully integrated manufacturing operation in Japan as quickly as possible. In pursuit of this goal Ford's Dearborn headquarters near Detroit approved the request to buy an eighty-two-acre plot of land in Yokohama but the sale was vetoed by the military. Ford's Japan boss at the time, Kopf, was convinced that the influence of Yoshisuke Aikawa, the head of the Nissan group, lay behind the army's obstructionism. Aikawa was close to the army, while Nissan formed a major part of the military's plan to establish a domestic auto industry.

Meanwhile, both GM and Ford had helped substantially to accelerate the development of a Japanese motor industry by sourcing parts locally. Mason relates how the American carmakers handed out for nominal fees details specifications of desired parts to Japanese components produces. These parts suppliers were to provide an invaluable infrastructure for Nissan and Toyota. Likewise, Ford and GM proved a great training ground for management personnel subsequently employed at the two major Japanese carmakers.

The noose continued to tighten on Ford and GM with a plethora of new regulations imposed by the military, including tight limits on production and strict foreign exchange controls. As business became increasingly impossible to pursue, Ford's Kopf tried vainly and belatedly to look for a Japanese merger partner. It proved to no avail because of the by then overt military hostility. Finally, with its Japanese assets effectively frozen, Ford appealed to the State Department in Washington to lobby the Japanese government to allow it to remit dividends and profits. In response, Finance Ministry officials informed Ford that if it wished to receive foreign exchange licenses it would have to buy ¥1 million worth of "China Incident" bonds, which had been issued to finance Japanese military forces' activities in Manchuria. Ford duly obliged. Yet even this act of naked appeasement did not work and by the end of the 1930s most of the company's foreign employees had left the country.

Ford and GM were the victims not only of a hostile military but also of active lobbying by both Nissan and Toyota that pressed for government assistance and protection as they developed their own manufacturing capabilities. Interestingly, restrictions on foreign direct investment continued to be supported after the war not only by Japanese officialdom but also, at least on a temporary basis, by paternalistic American Occupation authorities. They were concerned that foreign companies would take undue advantage of weakened and therefore temporarily vulnerable Japanese firms. This prevented some American companies from reentering the Japanese market as quickly as they might have wished. However, this was not the case for the Detroit carmakers. Both Ford and GM decided of their own accord not to go back into the Japanese domestic market immediately after the war because they did not then foresee the potential of the Japanese motor industry. This decision seems to have been taken regardless of the regulatory environment concerning foreign direct investment. Mason quotes what with the benefit of hindsight are two memorable internal memos. Thus, Ford International vice president Arthur Wieland wrote to Henry Ford II before the end of the Occupation as follows: "I presently cannot foresee any major competition from the Japanese motor automobile industry anywhere in the world outside Japan with the exception of China, Manchuria and Korea." Likewise at a critical meeting of GM's overseas policy group, top managers were told that "market potential at present or for the foreseeable future does not justify General Motors' consideration of undertaking local manufacture [in Japan]".

The American automakers' historical experience in Japan is not without significance when critics attack them for a lack of long-term commitment. For not only did they have an almost total grip on the domestic market before they were forced out of the country but their experience is also a salutary reminder that for much of its history Japan has had major restrictions on foreign direct investment. By the time these restrictions were properly lifted in the postwar era the cost of entry had already become a major issue. And now when asset prices have collapsed, making Japan in theory a much cheaper place for foreign companies to invest in, official policy seems hell-bent on preventing land and stock prices from clearing.

So the foreign direct investment issue is certainly not some fringe academic topic of interest only to learned professors. Rather it is probably the key issue in the long-simmering debate regarding Japan and its merchandise trade surplus. Yet so far the subject has only merited for the most part quasi-footnote status in the bilateral framework agreement compared with the Clinton administration's enduring obsession about reducing Japan's trade surplus to an arbitrary percentage of the GNP. This is most unfortunate if not plain absurd. For what is at stake here is both providing a nonprotectionist policy alternative to a very real political problem, which is the sheer size of Japan's surplus with all its major trading partners, but also at the same time reversing the direct investment gap that is substantially the consequence of Japan's past comparative economic isolation.

The Japanese government also has its part to play. It needs to do something because the low level of foreign direct investment in Japan is fast emerging as a de facto trade issue. Yet to date the Japanese government has shown scant awareness of the growing recognition among experts that, contrary to conventional economic theory, trade does follow investment, whereas previously the two were regarded as separate. The MITI white paper on trade, for example, barely contains a reference to foreign direct investment in Japan. This is of concern because so long as this attitude persists Japan will remain vulnerable to legitimate charges that it is not fully integrated in the world economy. David Hale, an economist with Chicago-based Kemper Financial Services, has pointed out that the flow of foreign direct investment into a country is a great way of causing that country to become a self-interested supporter of open-market policies by making it a more truly integrated member of the global economy. Thus, Hale writes with reference to contemporary France's high ambivalent attitude toward free trade: "Imagine how different French trade policy would be if it had as large a direct investment in east-

ern Europe and the former Soviet Union today as it had before the First World War when Russian bonds accounted for
over half of French external assets."* Imagine indeed.

Still, if more foreign direct investment provides the best
solution to the ever more glaring acrimony between Japan
and America over trade, the reality on the ground is that the
world is moving inexorably toward regional trading blocs regardless of politicians' pro-GATT rhetoric at events like the
Tokyo G7 summit. The North American Free Trade Agreement (NAFTA) area is only the most obvious example of this
trend, which is well described by Jagdish Bhagwati, a Colum-
bia University professor and one of the more eloquent de-
fenders of the virtues of free trade at a time when too many
free traders are on the run. He writes: "Today the enthusiasm
for regional free trade areas is dressed up as a great free trade
move. But it is evident that the main motivation is protectionist: Mexico becomes America's preferential market, with
Japan and the European Community at a disadvantage. . . .
As long as the talk of 'head to head' confrontation with the
European Community and Japan drives U.S. policy—with its
zero sum implication that their success means American failure—Washington will move towards preferential trading arrangements. As it pushes yet further into South America,
Washington will certainly provoke an Asian trading bloc."†

This is exactly what is happening. The Japanese may not
have announced a formal timetable to set up an Asian trading
bloc, as have the Europeans and continental Americans. But
both businessmen and bureaucrats have already long ago concluded that the world is moving toward a more regionally
based trading system that it is necessary to adapt to and prepare for. The result is an increasingly overt strategic retreat
back to Asia. This process has been further accelerated by the

* *"Can Japan Improve Its Trade Relations by Reforming Its Asset Markets?" (The Center for the Study of Financial Markets)*.
† Foreign Affairs, *Spring 1993*.

strength of the yen in the first half of 1993, which makes it cheaper for Japanese companies to install manufacturing facilities in Asia.

The yen's rise has another more dramatic effect. It makes it increasingly hard to justify in cost terms the manufacture of goods for export purposes in Japan. For very few Japanese exporters can make money at a level of ¥100 to the dollar, probably less than 5 percent. This can only lead to the growing move by Japanese manufacturers to escape soaring domestic unit-labor costs, up 21 percent between the beginning of 1991 and the beginning of 1993, by moving production abroad. The favored refuge will be mainland Asia and, in particular, China.

There is a lot of hollowing out to do because, compared with its industrial competitors, Japan still makes a high proportion of its products at home. Only 9 percent of manufacturing industry's total productive capacity was located outside Japan at the end of 1991, whereas the proportion for American industry is two to three times bigger. Naturally foreign direct investment out of Japan has collapsed in recent years, the consequence of the post-Bubble squeeze and plunging profits. Foreign direct investment totaled $17 billion in 1992, according to the Nomura Research Institute. Still, within this overall figure Asia's share has grown, a trend that will surely continue. Japanese companies invested $6.4 billion in Asia in the year to March 1993, compared with $5.9 billion the year before. Investment in China nearly doubled, though from a low base; from $579 million to $1.07 billion. Asia accounted for 19 percent of Japan's outstanding foreign direct investment in March 1993, up from 12 percent in 1990. By contrast, the shares of America and Europe have fallen from 46 percent to 40.5 percent and from 25 percent to 21 percent, respectively, over the same period.

A survey of Japanese companies published in 1993 by the Export-Import Bank of Japan suggests this trend will continue. Alongside the traditional bait of low labor costs and the unspoken one of the growing reality of regional trading blocs, Japanese companies can now see another compelling motive for investing in Asia. That is producing goods for local consumer markets. These markets are not sufficiently developed yet to absorb all the goods produced as a result of the excess capacity built during Japanese industry's late 1980s investment binge. Still, if they will not bail Japanese industry out of its immediate early 1990s' problems, these Asian markets offer huge medium-term potential as the consumers there become more affluent. Already in the countries belonging to the Association of Southeast Asian Nations, 64 percent of the existing subsidiaries of Japanese companies polled in the Ex-Im Bank survey and 56 percent of those planning projects aim to sell their products locally. China is now most in vogue among would-be investors, reflecting the intensity of that country's early 1990s economic boom. The survey lists it as the most favored country for future investment despite the all too obvious political risks. Traditional Japanese concerns about the productivity of the workforce, not to mention the sheer lawlessness in parts of China, especially the south, have for now it seems been outweighed by growing optimism about the potential for the consumer market. Japanese companies also seem to be shifting production away from relatively high-cost Malaysia and Thailand to Indonesia, the second favored country in the Ex-Im Bank survey and already a major beneficiary of Japanese investment, and even the Philippines. This is also a matter of balance. From a purely security point of view Japan has no wish to see political instability in any neighboring Asian country. Flows of Japanese capital are one way of preventing such instability by providing jobs and so the ability to generate wealth. This could mean that a country like the Philippines could hope to receive more investment in the future if it achieves a degree of credible political stability. In terms of its regional portfolio of direct investment, Japan had a total of $7.5 billion invested in Singapore at the end of September 1992, $4.6 billion in Malaysia, $5.5 billion in Thailand, $1.1 billion in the Philippines, $13.4 billion in Indonesia and $3.8 billion in China.

Japanese companies' investments in Asia have also been more profitable than those made in America and Europe. During the 1980s Japanese firms often built factories in America or Europe as a hedge against protectionism. In Asia the main driving force has always been a healthier one, namely the pursuit of profit. The electronics industry has so far led the move into Asian production, which is why the date will not be far off when no video recorders are manufactured for export in Japan. Mitsubishi Electronics already makes all its exportable video recorders in Southeast Asia. Out of Matsushita's total overseas production, Asia accounted at the end of 1992 for 61 percent, up from 49 percent in 1985. Matsushita has fifty-two manufacturing operations in Asia, including seven in China, which is likely to be the focus of the company's future expansion.

Carmakers have so far been more cautious, mainly because fewer Asian consumers can afford to buy cars than they can air conditioners and video recorders. But that is changing fast. By April 1993 Japanese car exports to America were only 2.2 times higher than its car exports to Asia. As late as March 1992 they were five times higher. By the end of 1994 on present trends Japanese car exports to Asia should be greater than those to America. With this burgeoning demand in the region it seems only a matter of time and perhaps more important affordability in terms of the carmakers' ability to pay for it before more Japanese car-making plants are constructed in Asia. Toyota already has announced plans to double its production in Thailand by 1997 while Nissan is now actively considering a plant in northern China. Japanese companies will sensibly avoid the economic hothouse of southern China where bust seems bound to follow such an uncontrollable boom, where labor is more expensive and where the general state of near anarchy is a real concern. Instead they will prefer to locate their plants in Manchuria, an area already familiar to major Japanese companies like Nissan for historical reasons.

However, the Japanese move into Asia will not be so swift as pure economic logic might suggest so long as Japan's major corporations remain faithful to the nostrum of lifetime employment. Consider the following: an unskilled production worker in Japan receives around ¥100,000 a month; his equivalent in Hanoi takes home perhaps $35. Yet Japanese companies still in practice like to hoard labor at home, the result more of adherence to lifetime employment than any enduring belief in a mythical labor shortage. A really precipitous hollowing out of Japan, which may well happen if Japanese companies choose to abandon the post-1945 employment system since the commercial logic is so compelling, would imply a dramatic psychological adjustment for which employees and indeed government are not yet ready. But it would have dramatic benefits for many Japanese firms' profit-and-loss accounts.

The growing focus of Japanese business on Asia has implications in the diplomatic and strategic fields as well, which Japanese policymakers are only now beginning to focus upon. It is also linked to the very fundamental question of whether Japan should continue to look to America for its defense umbrella and its major export market, or whether it should switch focus primarily to Asia and in particular China, a development that would naturally lead it increasingly to take care of its own security needs. Such questions represent one major (though long conveniently ignored) ideological fault line within the Liberal Democratic Party. They will have to be confronted soon, however.

Such is clear from the new post–Cold War reality in Asia. There can be no doubt now that Asia is an economic success story. Countless conferences have been held proclaiming the

"Pacific Rim century" or the "Asian miracle" to the extent that such slogans have been reduced to irritating clichés, mouthed by the same sort of superficially plausible people who gave overpaid lectures during the late 1980s telling the Western world they should convert to Japanese management practices in business just when those methods were in the process of failing on a spectacular scale.

Many Asian countries may have experienced spectacular growth rates in the past and do represent fast-growing consumer markets for the future as their middle class grows in size and affluence. Still, the reality of Asia, or rather East Asia, which is the region that most concerns Japan, is vastly more complicated than the trendy slogans suggest. For the end of the Cold War inevitably means the retreat of America's military presence, be it slow or precipitously fast, and in the resulting vacuum the rise of balance-of-power politics along the model of nineteenth-century Europe.

Many Asian "experts" still do not understand this because they have gotten used to peace and political stability in Asia since the end of the Vietnam War apart from the festering sore in Cambodia. Yet to assume that East Asia will remain purely a selection of countries populated by hardworking economic animals not given to dangerous political squabbling, let alone military conflict, is dangerously to ignore the message of history. Take, for example, the Asian colossus whose economic and political fortunes will shape the future development of the region. That is China. The early 1990s saw growing global euphoria, especially in America, concerning China's prospects in stark contrast to the dark mood that prevailed following the bloodshed in Tianamen Square. True, China or at least certain regions of the country, did experience rapid economic growth. The problem was, however, that the boom was so extreme that it showed every indication of ending in an equally dramatic bust. Indeed, southern China was in the midst of a bubblelike boom in early 1993 every bit as exaggerated as that which gripped Japan in the late 1980s. By the middle of 1993 the danger of overheating had finally become obvious to an increasingly nervous communist leadership. The issue was whether they had the means to control it. Thus, China's real GDP soared by an annualized 14 percent in the first three months of 1993, retail sales rose by 16 percent, and fixed investment by state enterprises expanded by an extraordinary 71 percent. Inflation was also rocketing, which was not surprising given annual 30 percent rates of money supply growth in the preceding three years. Anticipating hyperinflation, ordinary Chinese people were prepared to buy gold at prices substantially above the world market price as the best available hedge against a depreciating yuan. Meanwhile, much of the investment that has been undertaken will doubtless prove, as was the case in the recent past for Japan, grossly unproductive. Two thirds of China's fixed-asset investment is absorbed by state enterprises, most of whom produce products for which there is no demand.

China's boom can be correctly called the South China Bubble since this is the area where economic activity is most overheated and where there has been the greatest breakdown of law and order with the atmosphere more akin to the Wild West than a communist police state. All this is deeply destabilizing on a national level. First, fraud and corruption have risen exponentially, which is bound to generate social tensions. Second, it is not a stable situation when one part of a country is growing at annual rates of perhaps 30 percent while other more rural regions are barely growing at all. This anomaly, combined with the rising inflationary pressures, explain evidence of mounting discontent in the countryside. Peasant riots in the middle of 1993 were the final signal to the nervous Beijing authorities that they had to crack down with strict credit controls and the like. Whether they can succeed and enforce their authority will decide whether the communist regime survives. For if they fail in the task, which is likely, the boom will become ever more fevered in the short term with a corresponding even greater bust later. China could then be split further apart by the forces pushing for greater local autonomy or still worse by outright civil war. China has an unfortunate history of intermittent bouts of anarchy.

Japan's leaders are well aware of this risk of political instability since China has long been their neighbor. As a result, Japanese businessmen have not been caught up in the euphoria that has caused many American and European companies, not to mention overseas Chinese, to invest in China in such reckless fashion. For when the inevitable bust happens, coinciding with the equally inevitable political fallout, many of those same investors are likely to retreat in shock when they realize that China is not immediately about to deliver on its promise of becoming a giant consumer market ready and willing to buy all their products.

Japan's leadership will also be forced to address another aspect of current Chinese government policy. That is its growing defense spending as China aspires to great power status. China's defense spending has been growing at double-digit rates in real terms in the early 1990s with Beijing happy to take advantage of the Russians' willingness to sell weapons for hard cash. But if China offers a potential military threat in the medium term, the clear short-term threat to Japan's security comes from the north of the Korean peninsula. This is the area Japan's strategic thinkers are now most focused on. Minds were concentrated when on May 29, 1993, North Korea successfully test-fired a modified Scud missile, the Nodong 1, which with a one-thousand-kilometer range can reach targets in Japan. This has raised real concerns in Tokyo that Japan is unable to defend itself against high-altitude missile attacks that could conceivably carry the nuclear warheads that the world suspects the North Koreans of developing. This may seem far-fetched. But given the history of the North Korean regime, for example, the assassination of much of the South

Korean cabinet in a bomb blast in Rangoon in the early 1980s, the Japanese are not prepared to grant the benefit of the doubt. This is why Japan's defense establishment is now considering a Theater Missile Defense System, a form of technology developed as part of America's "Star Wars" or Strategic Defense Initiative. This is a first move in what will inevitably result at some point in a Japanese arms buildup, a development that will involve the purchase of American technology. For even if the North Korean regime has collapsed by the time this book is published, a unified Korean peninsula will in itself present a strategic threat that Japan will not be able to ignore, given the history of excessive acrimony between the two countries. Demographics alone dictates this. Projecting forward present birth rates, Daewoo Research Institute estimates there will be 85 million Koreans compared with 129 million Japanese by the year 2010. Yet as recently as 1980 there were only 56 million Koreans compared with 117 million Japanese.

The Chinese and Korean examples, not to mention the reemergence at some time in the future of a hostile Russia, are all powerful reasons why Japanese politicians, however reluctantly, will be forced to abandon the defense strategy that has persisted since the Second World War. That is a defense arsenal which has been aimed exclusively north at a perceived Russian threat to Hokkaido, Japan's northern island.

Clearly how quickly Japan rearms will depend most, in the absence of nasty shocks, on American policy in the region. If Americans abandoned all responsibility for Asian security, Japan's rearmament would be extremely rapid. But even if the withdrawal is more gradual, as still remains more likely despite mounting isolationist sentiment in Washington, the hard geographic facts combined with the end of the Cold War dictate a fundamental change in Japan's strategic thinking. For Japan is a vulnerable island nation whose resource-dependent economy can be closed down in a matter of weeks by a hostile power with the naval power to block shipping lanes. This is not a situation any responsible Japanese political leader, with his country's national interest to defend, could tolerate if he had any doubts at all about the strength of the American commitment. And indeed many of Japan's more nationalistic politicians would argue it is not a situation that should ever have been tolerated regardless of the stated American commitment, strong or weak.

There is also another factor that will make an arms buildup increasingly tempting. That is the moribund economy. Arms spending will be one sure way of helping revive an economy that will continue to disappoint officialdom's expectations. The sort of high-tech electronic defense missile systems that Japan will need to bolster its defense effort will also in large part be imported from America, which should help the trade statistics. The question is not therefore if Japan's defense policy will change but rather when it will happen and how rapid will be the subsequent rearmament.

Astonishingly, such points appear to remain lost on the official guardians of Japan's foreign policy. That is the Ministry of Foreign Affairs or *gaimesho*. Its attentions remain focused on one key foreign policy goal. That is Japan attaining a permanent seat on the United Nations Security Council. This may be a worthy aim to which Japan has every reason to aspire given its economic clout, but it should hardly be the be-all and end-all of diplomatic policy as it often appears to be. By contrast the hard questions about what the end of the Cold War means for Asia's complex and delicate balance of power, about who will in the future police the region, are seldom acknowledged as issues, let alone openly discussed. The worry is that the internationalist side of Japan, symbolized by Foreign Ministry types who strongly support the American alliance and the post-1945 status quo as expressed in the obsession with a seat on the Security Council, will lose the convergence argument because they will not be prepared when there are calls made for a more nationally assertive Japan in military policy. Their quiescent attitude also reflects a dangerous dependence on big brother America. Buruma has written: "The present relationship between the U.S. and Japan is an unhealthy one. Japan is a resentful and mercantilist power locked into a state of infantile dependence on U.S. security."* This curious situation will not last in the new Japan.

If it is clear that the post-1945 consensus about Japan's foreign policy will have to change, shaped as it will be by trade and defense considerations, it is far from clear what will emerge out of the resulting vacuum. A responsible Japanese defense buildup would be understandable given the post–Cold War realities. A precipitous buildup, combined with an aggressive regional economic focus, would cause alarm bells to ring everywhere.

* New York Review of Books, *March 25, 1993.*

Epilogue

THE SHEER ENORMITY of the structural crisis facing Japan became even clearer in the first few months of 1994. What is at stake here is no cyclical blip but a sea change in the way an entire society is run. Radical change is coming and it will come fast because of the crushing pressure of a high yen and a deflating economy.

Politically, the situation has gone from bad to worse. The fall of the Hosokawa government in April precipitated by renewed attention over Mr. Hosokawa's links with the scandal-plagued moving company Sagawa Kyubin was yet another reminder that the mold in Japanese politics has been broken. True, Hosokawa did succeed during his premiership in pushing through reform of the electoral system. However, he proved no apostle of change. Political reform was about the only issue on which Mr. Hosokawa's coalition government's diverse members could agree. Relations with America also steadily deteriorated over the trade issue during his period as prime minister. A sentimental nationalist who preferred Asia's ways to those of the West, Hosokawa was not comfortable negotiating with the United States. Meanwhile, the economic news has remained almost overwhelmingly negative, a trend helped by the Clinton administration's continued insistence on talking up the yen. The Japanese currency is back to trading around its all-time highs, near ¥100 to the dollar. The Japanese currency is now as overvalued as the dollar was in 1984 prior to the following year's Plaza Accord.

The continued strength of the yen is putting intolerable pressure on the manufacturing sector to the point where Japan's industrial base is now threatened. The decline in Japanese manufacturing has already been far greater than most observers realize. Japan's trade surplus on manufactured goods, measured as a ratio of the country's GNP, has nearly halved since 1985 when the yen began its ascent, declining from 9.7 percent to 5.3 percent in 1993. Economic data also continue to show an astonishing loss of competitiveness vis-a-vis America. Between 1985 and 1993 manufacturing production increased by 25 percent in America compared with only 11 percent in Japan. Yet, during the same period, manufacturing employment declined by 8 percent in America and rose by 7 percent in Japan. As a result, American productivity improved by 35 percent whereas Japanese productivity rose by only 4 percent.

The unpalatable result is that unless the yen weakens soon, scrapping of excess production capacity in Japan will take place on a very large scale with employees released onto the labor market much quicker than the service industries will be able to absorb them. For the ability of the corporate sector to continue to act as an unofficial welfare state, subsidizing more than 3 million underemployed workers becomes harder to sustain by the day. Yet, the question of how to handle the colossal restructuring task now confronting the Japanese economy, in terms of the dramatic reallocation of human resources that is entailed, continues to be ignored by politicians and bureaucrats alike.

The employment issue will soon come to a boil, though, since the financial pressures are so severe. Nomura Research Institute, hardly an extremist organization, forecast in December 1993 a decline in GNP growth in 1994 and, perhaps worse, an astonishing fifth consecutive year of declining profits for Japanese companies in the financial year that began in April 1994. The key problems remain the weakness in private capital spending and consumption which together account for about 80 percent of the Japanese economy. Capital spending will continue to fall in both the manufacturing and nonmanufacturing sectors in 1994 and probably in 1995 as well, while consumption will be an obvious victim of any crack in the employment system. Japan's unemployment rate would probably already be 7 to 8 percent rather than the current 2.9 percent if the totem of lifetime employment had already been abandoned. It soon will be, since the rigid employment system has become perhaps the major obstacle for a Japanese economy that needs to respond more quickly to the competitive challenges posed by a world economy moving fast into the information age.

If Japan does not rise to this challenge, the country risks sharing the fate of America's IBM. And there are notable similarities between this former industrial powerhouse of an economy and the shrunken American corporate giant besides their long-shared adherence to paternalistic employment systems. Five years ago, IBM was too wedded to its own traditional belief systems to recognize the threat posed to its continued survival by fast changing events in the outside world. After indulging in the absurd arrogance of the late 1980s Bubble, Japan's iron triangle of bureaucrats, businessmen and politicians has been equally slow in the 1990s to acknowledge the impending inevitability of deep structural change. For the old ways no longer work. This time is really different.

Still, there are glimmers of progress. It is now clear that there are voices within both the bureaucracy and the ranks of politicians, not to mention the business community, calling for structural change. Such people argue correctly that the swiftest way out of Japan's present morass is to let prices clear and to allow loss-making entities to be liquidated so that new capital can be invested in new business ventures at prices that make economic sense. Naturally, such a transition means much pain, turmoil and uncertainty in a society not accustomed to these sorts of conditions. But creative destruction and regeneration is the only way forward. The alternative is continued logjam and continued denial.

The financial markets have sent a mixed message. A less committed government support operation combined with an intensifying unwinding of the doomed cross-shareholding system caused a renewed slide in the Nikkei back to the 16,000 level in late 1993, again raising concerns about the health of the financial system. But the foreigners once more rescued Japan from the brink of financial catastrophe by purchasing an astonishing $35 billion worth of Japanese shares in the first three months of 1994. The foreigners' enthusiasm reflected in part their naive conviction that the employment system would hold and the political problems would prove short-lived, and in part their desire to divert money out of the overvalued markets of Southeast Asia into "cheap" Japan. Still, the Japanese stock market remains a high-risk area in the absence of any improvement in corporate earnings, supported as it is at the margin by fickle foreign buying. Meanwhile, the property market remains as depressed as it is illiquid. The liquidation in Japanese real estate when it finally occurs will be extremely vicious since prices are by now already some 70 percent down from their late 1980s peak levels.

The banking sector has also continued to fail to perform its proper function, the extension of credit, as a result of the prevailing wait-and-see attitude toward the bad-debt problem. Outstanding loans at Japan's city banks fell by nearly one percent between April and September 1993, the first time this has happened since such data began to be accumulated. Perhaps even more astonishing, Lehman Brothers, an American investment bank, has noted that, based on the latest available data, public sector institutions in 1993 were larger new lenders to the private sector than were private financial institutions, an anomalous situation that might be described as socialism by default. Such a paralyzed banking system explains why the Finance Ministry is now engaged in a fierce internal debate about whether to allow the bad-debt problem to be liquidated, an approach that would enable Japan to make use of the established American technique of securitization. This makes perfect sense in theory. A practical problem, though, is that in order to be successful, securitization requires total transparency since buyers of a loan converted into a security want to know exactly what they are buying. This is not always possible in Japan because title to a property is often pledged many times over while many of the banking system's nonperforming loans are owned by *yakuza* interests.

One point is clear. When the liquidation occurs, it will prove especially traumatic precisely because the marking-to-market process will be so unusual in the Japanese context. Japan Inc. became so arrogant in the late 1980s because it really believed it was immune from the natural laws of the marketplace. This really was one of the most astonishing acts of mass delusion ever, and future historians, be they Japanese or *gaijin*, will marvel at it. Yet, because the belief was held so universally across all strata of society, the resulting collision with reality will be that much more painful. Catharsis is ultimately a healing process. But only if the subject can handle the strain.

This raises the key question of the political response to the inevitability of rising unemployment. The nature of that response, and the nature of the political debate that precedes it, will shape the course taken by the new Japan. During this process there will be increasingly open ideological political conflict. This will be shocking to many Japanese people who have been brought up to believe that such conflict occurs only in the West. Such a cozy assumption will prove a delusion. Indeed, it is based on profound historical ignorance. There was, for example, great ideological conflict over economic policy in Japan during the 1920s and 1930s, as described in the epilogue of my last book.*

Ideological conflict will occur again over the social reality of rising unemployment and what to do about it. The fact that the bureaucracy is already internally debating the issue of liquidation shows that officialdom is moving, however slowly and however reluctantly, to some form of market resolution of Japan's crisis. Applied to the corporate sector, this approach means sanctioning widespread layoffs—certainly a painful process. But it is not all bad news. For the jobs displaced will be replaced by new jobs in new industries serving different needs. Long overdue deregulation in sectors like real estate, retailing and agriculture will lead to the emergence of new growth markets. The leisure industry is just one example of an industry with enormous potential. The Japanese people as individual consumers will probably lead a better life both in terms of the amount of free time at their disposal and in terms of what their money will buy them. Japan will become a consumerist society with all the diversity of choice long taken for granted by spoiled Americans.

But this is the positive medium-term picture. In the shorter term, rising unemployment risks provoking widespread anger because from the salaried worker's point of view, such a turn of events is simply not meant to happen. It is not on the radar screen of his registered consciousness. As bad, the average employee never enjoyed the full prosperity of the Bubble and may now suffer personally from its bursting. The resulting rise in social friction, which should not be underestimated as the social contract is rent assunder, will pose a major test of public policy. Japan has little tradition of insti-

* The Bubble Economy, pp. 206–10.

tutionalized social welfare, with that role usually played by the family or the company. There is certainly no decent institutional mechanism in place for dealing with the scale of the likely coming employment adjustment.

The political debate will revolve around whether the cost of unemployment should be socialized with labor subsidies, welfare schemes and the like, or whether the burden should be placed on the traditional family structure financed by the Japanese people's still high savings rate. This debate will split the coalition government formed by Hata (who replaced Hosokawa as prime minister) and result in the emergence of two right-wing parties: one representing a more classic free-market, American-style, pro-business approach and the other more ambivalent about economic growth, more pro-bureaucracy and Asian-centric, paternalistic with a strong sense of Japan's uniqueness and a general bias in favor of regulation. Similar ideological conflict will occur over foreign policy where the new Japan will have to address the new geopolitical strategic realities of Asia, be it a re-arming of China, a more distant if not plain hostile U.S.–Japan relationship, uncertainty at best in the Korean peninsula, and the possible reemergence of a hostile Russia.

Out of this ideological debate a new consensus will eventually emerge after perhaps another five years of drift, instability and weak governments. Japan is not a country able to tolerate weak government for long. But first the argument must be joined. The Japanese people should prepare for a rocky ride, as should Japan's trade partners and regional neighbors. The old certainties have gone. And for the moment there is nothing to take their place.

—May 1994

Index